Trusting the Healer Within

BY NICK BAMFORTH

Author of *Aids and the Healer Within*

AMETHYST BOOKS

NEW YORK   LONDON

This book is dedicated to the nursing profession for their unheralded love, compassion and devotion.

Published in the United States by Amethyst Books, P.O. Box 895, Woodstock, N.Y. 12498
and in the United Kingdom by Amethyst Books, 44 Gledstanes Road, London W14

Designed by Paperweight

Library of Contress Catalog Card Number: 88–83320

ISBN 0–944256–04–X

Amethyst Books are distributed in the United States by Publishers Group West, 4065 Hollis, Emeryville, CA 94608 and in the United Kingdom by Ashgrove Distribution, 4 Brassmill Centre, Brassmill Lane, Bath BA1 3JN.

Trusting
the
Healer
Within

Contents

Introduction   7

1 Understanding the Healer Within 11

Trust and Faith   13
Life and Death   21
Children and Parents   31
The Physical and the Spiritual   38
The Endocrine System   43
The Seven Chakras   50
The Chakras and Our Physical Anatomy   54

2 Practicing the Healer Within   61

The Physical, the Earth and the First Chakra   63
   Meditation No. 1
Sex   73
   Meditation No. 2
Sexuality: the Male and Female Within All of Us   83
Emotions and Pain   88
Forgiveness   95
   Meditation No. 3
Sorrow, Grief and Bereavement   99

Meditation No. 4
Fear   106
Creativity and Limitation   111
Meditation No. 5
The Third Chakra: the Seat of the Ego   115
Control   119
Meditation No. 6
Judgment and Guilt   126
Meditation No. 7 Addiction and Isolation   133
Strength and Faith   139
Meditation No. 8
The Fourth Chakra: the Heart Center   145
Relationships   147
Love: the Great Healer   152
The Fifth Chakra: Communication and
Expression   155
The Power of Words   157
Meditation No. 9
The Sixth Chakra: the Rational and the Intuitive   162
Meditation No. 10

Postscript   171

Introduction

Since the publication of my book, *AIDS & The Healer Within*, so many people have told me that what I wrote applied equally to any other disease and obstacle we encounter in our lives and that I should therefore write another broader based book – not just on health and disease, but also on other aspects of our personal growth.

What has finally persuaded me to go ahead with this is that, in the intervening year, I myself have gone through such profound changes that my understanding of the dynamics of change in our inner and outer lives could not help but become clearer, and I feel that I have so much to add to what I wrote only a year ago.

For, without doubt, we have just entered into a period of change more powerful than at any time in living memory. For years, a momentous energy has been building up in our inner lives and in the outer workings of our planet, and this has now been released with a surge which will not fail to touch the existence of a single person living today. Whatever you call this new era into which we are entering, the important thing is to really allow yourself to feel and understand the emotions which the prospect of profound change arouses in you: whether ones of fear or of eager anticipation. Part of the aim of this book is to enable you to learn faith and allow yourself to be carried forward in peace and harmony by this new energy.

For myself, all my closest friends and, I suspect, most of you reading this book, the past few years have been the most intense of our lives. Within this intensity, there has been a great deal of sorrow and pain, and I know only too well how it feels to experience those times when, despite all the work you are doing on yourself, there seems to be no light at the end of the tunnel.

If I had not experienced such extremes of emotion in my own life, I would not be in a position to write this book. I have been fortunate to have always had that spark of trust and faith, however faint, during even the darkest periods of my life, and I have always understood that even the deepest feelings of pain and loss were there to stimulate me towards a new stage of growth and change. I find, nowadays, that each time something knocks me into a hole, I learn the lesson and climb out of it more quickly with a feeling of lightness at the end. In the past six months, I have undergone the experience of severely spraining my ankle and the excruciating pain of passing a kidney stone – as I shall illustrate later, each of these had a specific message for me, which ultimately helped to release certain elements within my own behavior which were holding me back from my highest good.

Of course, I realize that it is not always that easy for all of us to instantly learn from an intense experience and then put the pain of it behind us. One thing that the kidney stone was there to remind me of was that pain – whether physical, emotional or that fear when confronted with a life-threatening disease – can be all-consuming, so that there appears to be no room for anything else in your mind and body. But, once that original all-consuming intensity wears off and there is finally space for some other sensation, this is where the real challenge begins: whether to take charge or to give in, whether to actively participate in your own healing process or passively rely on outside forces to buffet you around. It is a very basic choice.

This is fundamentally what this book is all about. We are constantly confronted with fundamental choices and the major decisions we make govern the course of our lives.

When we are confronted with a dis-ease, this is a means of bringing us face to face with our inner being and examining what it is that is blocking the flow of our existence. It is at such critical points in our lives that we are presented with the greatest opportunity to grow and create transformation within ourselves.

For me to say that our health and well-being are our own responsibility in no way implies blame or guilt if we are sick or in pain. For all of us, periods of sickness and inner pain provide the impetus for us to set out on a new path, a path with infinite possibilities. If we were not to go through such intense experiences, our lives would be static and we would never learn or grow.

The purpose of this book is twofold. The first part is to enable you to understand the process by which dis-ease stimulates growth and change within you. The second part guides you, in a practical way, towards achieving such growth and inner transformation.

Before you do continue, however, I would like to stress that this course of self-healing is in no way meant to replace any medication which you may be taking if you have a physical disease. It is always a matter of personal choice whether or not one follows the advice of one's doctor concerning medical treatment. As far as I am concerned, the only fundamental decision in this respect is whether a patient actively participates in his or her healing or passively relies on medicine to 'cure' the disease.

Also, to complement the search for inner balance and harmony which is the focus of this book, I always recommend that all of us should be very aware of our physical bodies. This includes regular physical exercize and a nutritious, balanced diet. If there is a serious disease involved, I always suggest that the person in question undergoes a thorough nutritional check-up, such as a hair test, which highlights any major sources of allergic, nutritional imbalance within the body.

1

Understanding the Healer Within

Trust and Faith

It's all very well talking about such abstract concepts as trust and faith, you may say, but what exactly do these words mean and what significance do they have in our day to day lives?

The answer rests in the philosophy and sense of spirit which lie behind this book and which are fundamental to my own actions as I go through my own day to day life. In a sense, by defining this, I am beginning at the end, as the aim of this book is to teach you, the reader, to attain the faith and trust in your own ability to heal your life and take responsibility for each and every one of your actions and thoughts. Yet, without understanding what it is you are aiming for, the whole exercise may seem somewhat pointless.

This is why this first section, 'Understanding The Healer Within', is important, for without this understanding, or, more to the point, a strong intuitive feel for it, there is no impetus for you to put it into practice.

From a very early age, through the educational system to our first job and onwards, the emphasis of our lives in the Western world is primarily on achievement and on fitting in to certain patterns and modes of behavior. Whether in careers or relationships, whether through the pressure of society or the continuous bombardment of advertising, there is a certain norm which is presented to us as the traditionally acceptable way of living and relating to the world around us. Some of us may accept this wholeheartedly in a conservative manner; others may rebel and forge a separate path of their own making.

However, to me, whether you are a conservative or a liberal, a traditionalist or a rebel is irrelevant. For this is the outer world, and the scope of this book is the inner world.

The inner world – the world of emotions, mind and spirit – is, for the individual, the only continuous and truly real world. The outer world – the world of physical reality, of careers, relationships, health, financial prosperity – is merely a reflection of the inner state of an individual, just as the physical state of this planet Earth is a reflection of the consciousness of those who live upon it.

For hundreds of years, this inner world was considered to be the realm of the many diverse religions which covered our planet. For many people, this is still the case, although science and psychology have also staked their claim, bringing the inner and outer closer together in the minds of men by means of explanations of this inner world in physical, rational, 'outer' terms.

Nowadays, the diversity of belief systems, philosophies, religions etc. seems to be almost endless and the conflict caused by intolerance towards conflicting viewpoints is only too evident throughout the world. Yet the one truth remains: we all have the ability to choose what we believe in. And that choice can only come from within: we may be given tangible evidence that this or that is correct, but, unless it *feels* right, we know deep down that it is not right *for us*. I stress 'for us', because every reality is subjective. What feels right to me does not necessarily feel right to you and vice-versa.

Which is why I have chosen to begin with the fundamentals of faith and trust as I see them. Only if they resonate with you will they give you the drive to explore this book further.

As I look back on the thirty-six years of my life, I now see how the long journey of ups and downs, pleasure and pain has fundamentally been a journey towards faith, with all else gradually falling away as I am confronted with one obstacle after another, one period of intense experience after another.

For many, the word faith is associated with people who do not use their rational powers and blindly follow some movement or religion that does all the thinking for them and takes away all sense of personal responsibility. Indeed, certain religions do continue to exist in this way, as the propagation of any dogma which lays down the limits of 'right' and 'wrong' is an incredible instrument of power. In claiming a higher authority, they can easily control and manipulate those who passively put their faith and trust in them.

Fortunately, or unfortunately, depending on the way you look at it, the faith and trust which I am writing about is not so easy.

Many of the religions of today, including Christianity, spread the notion of One Supreme Being or God which is above and totally separate from us. It is all at once a benevolent, devastating, omniscient being which sits in judgment over humanity and all living things. It has passed down to us certain rigid rules of conduct which are to be obeyed. It is the ultimate authority and the only choice open to man is whether or not to believe in and obey this authority.

It is no small wonder that the fundamentalists of any religion use this 'ultimate authority' to excuse their intolerance and hatred towards any belief system which strays even slightly from their own. This 'faith' is in essence a brick wall, an obstacle to any change within society or personal growth within an individual.

Yet, on the other side of the coin, there are, within any traditional religious movement, those individuals who live by their own conscience and guiding spirit and who spread an energy of love and compassion wherever they go, helping and guiding those who cross their path without judgment or blame. These are the beings who radiate the God within them in all their actions and it is they who are the true bearers of spirit and faith.

We are all part of a Universe whose size and diversity our minds are unable to fully grasp. Just as each cell in our body is a separate entity unto itself yet also an integral part of the body as a whole, we are individuals in our own right but equally an integral part of this Whole we call the Universe. Just as our lives are everchanging, so the formation and extent of the Universe are constantly fluid, due to the continuous transformation of the individual components within it.

We only have to look at the cycle of life and mutual dependency within nature to understand that everything within the world which we perceive is interdependent. Even as science becomes more refined, there is an increasing sense within the physicists and biologists of our time that there lies beneath all natural phenomena a sense of order and consistency which binds us all together – not the rigid, immutable order imposed upon us by a Supreme Being, but a fluid, free floating force within which there is always room for choice and change. The ONE, whether you call it God or the Universe or any other name, is that energy which binds us all together. Each and every one of us is part of that force, inseparable from it, yet with the choice and the free will to go our own way.

We are part of God, rather than separate from God.

Because we are part of God or the Universe, we can, through its infinite connections, bring this order, complete balance and harmony, into our own lives and ultimately help to bring it to the lives of others. We are all divine beings and we all have the capacity to tap into this limitless Universal Energy in order to carry us forward to our highest potential.

Of course, when we are confronted with a crisis or a particular low point in our existence, this connection to a Divine Energy seems tenuous to say the least. When everything is going wrong in your life, you are more likely to be shaking your fist at the 'injustice of God' or to be consumed by the dark, empty feeling that there is no such Divine Energy and that this 'painful' physical world is the only reality. Everyone, even the most enlightened spiritual teachers, has at some point in their lives gone through such deep troughs of doubt and darkness.

So, what of trust and faith? What relevance do they have when we are at the lowest ebb in our lives? How do they enable us to heal our lives?

The answer begins with our perception of what dis-ease is all about.

When I now look back on those periods of my life when I went through the most severe physical sickness, emotional distress or even a feeling of stagnation, of 'What's the point of it all?', I see that these were the times when I was really brought face to face with my own true essence.

In our modern existence, we are surrounded by material things, whether in terms of physical possessions or our desire for material success and security. There is so much clutter in our lives and this includes the emotional and psychological baggage we carry around with us too. We are constantly putting our energy out to supposedly enhance the quality of our lives in a material way, filling each moment of our existence with 'things to do', with specific material goals, with physical objects or past-times which fill the space around us and make us feel secure. Most of such behavior is prompted by need: the need to feel complete, to belong, to feel connected, anything to prevent us from feeling alone or bored. It is our rational mind which craves for things to occupy it.

Yet, there is another side to every human being, best summed up by that sense of awe we all feel when confronted by a scene of immense natural beauty, such as an incredible sunset or the view from the top of a mountain. It is the feeling that, even standing there alone, we are still connected to and belong to something greater and more powerful than our rational minds can begin to comprehend. It is also that part of us which understands deep down that all the physical things with which we surround ourselves are purely temporal in nature and have no real bearing on our lives. It is the knowledge that, when it comes down to the crunch, what really matter in our lives are our relationships with our fellow beings and with ourselves.

This is what I mean by our true essence: cutting away all the crap in our lives and understanding what is really important, what really matters. Anyone who is confronted with a life-threatening disease will know this feeling. If you see the possibility of your life upon this physical plane ending, past experiences tend to stream past your mind like a mirror and the present and future are laid out before you pared down to the bare essentials: 'What is it that I feel I have missed out on? What is it that I truly want from the time I have left?' Without knowing it, we live so much of our lives in fear, fear of taking risks, of doing things other people will disapprove of. When confronted with dis-ease and sometimes despair, we are dragged closer to that point where we are honest with ourselves and can find the courage to follow our true path.

Let us be truly honest with ourselves. Is this not what we all want? Do we not want to act true to ourselves rather than constantly making compromises and bowing to an authority and way of life that others have imposed upon us?

Faith is the knowledge that whatever we feel is right for us really is right for us. It is trusting that intuitive part of us which just knows when something is right or wrong. It is the understanding that such intuitive knowledge is our connection to that Universal Energy which will guide us towards our highest good as long as we keep the channel to It open. It is also trusting that dis-ease comes into our existence as a means of stimulating us to look deep within

18

ourselves, to change and to grow.

Trusting the Healer Within is the faith that we are part of rather than separate from God.

To attain that faith can be a long and arduous journey – I am the last to deny that. It is the gradual process of peeling the layers away, like those of an onion, until you reach the core which is your own true nature, that wonderful individual essence which is distinct from but also part of the Whole. It is the process of letting go of the notion that you have to control each tiny, intricate aspect of your life and learning to allow your intuition to see the whole picture and to guide you to make the really important decisions of your life.

And if such behavior seems unrealistically passive to you, just for a moment examine your philosophy of life and in particular your attitude towards control. Do you really believe that life is and must always be a continuous struggle? Do you feel that you have to keep everything in your life under control and does that hide a basic fear of losing control and being at the mercy of other people or 'cruel fate'? Are you governed by the belief that no one can be truly happy or fulfilled and that you just have to get by as best as you can?

If you answer 'yes' to any of these questions, I say that you are not fully entering into your true essence. You are only looking at half the picture, that rational part of you which will only see for yourself what appears to fit into your 'limitations'.

You are denying your *whole* nature which looks outwards and beyond the limits of the rational mind, which always needs proof and solid evidence before it steps gingerly forward.

You are surrendering to fear and allowing the infinite possibilities of life to pass you by.

Faith is certainly not passive. It means finding that stillness and balance within so that you can listen to that inner voice which guides you towards making the really important choices, which will in turn lead you towards your highest

19

potential. It means cutting away all the excess baggage which weighs you down and allowing yourself to be swept along your own chosen path, turning and changing at will.

It is the ultimate responsibility, because no one will tell you what to do or where to go. It is trusting that what you feel is right *is* right.

Life and Death

Of course, the ultimate fear for most people is the fear of death, for it is the fear of the end, the fear of the unknown and, most important, the fear of separation from all the people and the familiar things around us. It is the fear of the void, of nothingness.

We have all heard the common saying: 'The only one certain thing in our lives is that we shall die.' Yet, why is is that so few of us prepare for, let alone confront this real fact? Death, in our modern Western lives, is something which must be swept under the carpet, must always be discussed in the quietest, whispered tones – again, all as a result of fear.

Such fear is, once more, a result of our rational minds which do not see the ultimate truth behind the reality of our physical lives. The rational mind must see everything in sequence and there must always be a beginning and an end to everything. The extent of this beginning and end is the extent to which the rational mind can grasp something. Before Galileo came along with his telescope, the only reality was this planet Earth and the stars were seen as twinkling lights in the sky which revolved around us. In current scientific terms, DNA is the smallest decipherable code which passes on our genetic heritage, but this was only relatively recently discovered and there is little doubt that scientists will sooner or later discover some individual, more microscopic component of DNA itself.

By its very nature, the rational mind will never see the whole picture. It will strive to understand as much as it can, but always needs proof that something exists. And, of course, there are those, from the most brilliant scientist to the average man on the street, who will say: 'If no one can prove something to me, it is not real or true.' This philosophy is in itself an individual choice.

I cannot prove to you that we continue beyond physical death. It is only something you can feel within yourself. But, seriously, do you really believe that you go through the intensity and variety of experience and growth in this life and that it just ends?

Again, only you can answer this.

Let me return to those elements of fear which death inspires within us.

The fundamental fear, and the one which rules the way we live as well as the way we approach death, is the separation from what we have around us, from all that is 'familiar' to us. 'Better the devil you know than the one you don't know' is another popular saying, illustrating that need within us to cling on to what is familiar, even if it is something which brings us nothing but misery.

The people, the experiences, the things we have perceived with our five senses are all that our memory retains and it is therefore hardly surprising that this present physical life seems to be the only reality. The thrust of our lives is to make the best of this physical world for ourselves and our families. Our lives are structured upon the supposition that we will live approximately three score years and ten, or more. It is only when we grow old or are confronted with a life threatening disease in our 'prime' that most of us come face to face with death.

Whether or not we are happy and contented at this stage in our lives, we rarely welcome the prospect of our mortal existence coming to an end. We do not want to be separated from our loved ones; we feel that there is so much more to do before we go, etc.. In these physical terms, death does indeed mean the end; it seems to be something random over which we have no control and it has no respect for the wishes of whomever it strikes. It is an instrument of blind fate or an omnipotent God, whatever way you choose to look at it.

And beyond it, there is either nothing or heaven or hell, whichever way you wish to look at it.

You may feel here that I am being a little flippant about so serious a subject, but, by pointing out that all such attitudes towards life and death are perfectly understandable, I am making a very specific point.

If you look at the accepted values of modern society, there are three prevalent attitudes towards death. Firstly, there is the traditional religious view of Heaven and Hell, where one meets the judgment of almighty God. Secondly, there is the rational view that there is no proof of life after death and it therefore does not exist. Thirdly, there is that hopeful wavering somewhere between the two, where there is no strong belief, but 'there is no proof that there is no life after death'.

What all these three attitudes have in common is that they see that death is something separate from life, rather than an intergral part of it. In fact, they have nothing to do with life at all, as they are all totally passive. It is all very well controlling every aspect of your existence as long as you are alive on this physical plane, but does it not make a mockery of your whole life if you surrender just when you are confronted by the ultimate challenge and transformation which death represents?

The specific point is: do you want to live life to its fullest potential or not? Do you believe that you as you know yourself end for good when you die or at best are subject to judgement by a supreme being?

Or do you believe that this life is a stage within a continuous process of change, just as Nature, this Earth, the Universe are in a continuous state of flux and change? Do you or do you not sense that this physical world around us

23

is what is transitory? Do you not feel that what is permanent and never dying is that individual, inner part of you, whether you call it spirit, soul or whatever?

If you have not already done so, I ask you to confront this fundamental question before you continue with this book, because the way you approach death reflects the way you approach life. If you believe that physical death is the end or that your own input into your own existence ceases beyond death, then your attitude towards your life on this planet will necessarily be affected and you will therefore find it more difficult to mobilize the Healer Within.

As you will now understand, when I am writing about life, I am not just referring to the physical existence we lead and the day to day events in our lives, but the totality of life: the inner and the outer, the conscious and the subconscious. Running parallel to the external reality which we continuously experience is that internal reality which governs not only our thoughts and ultimately our actions, but which is also our fundamental link to our highest potential, our creativity and the great well of subconscious knowledge which is stored within ourselves and within the Universe as a whole.

This inner reality will often remain hidden for years within an individual until something major happens within that person's life, which stops them short and lights that spark which arouses the flame within. Throughout our lives, from childhood on, we are given glimpses of that 'other world' which expands far beyond our own little island of existence, but those glimpses are ignored or shoved aside for being 'irrelevant' or, more often, for fear of opening a can of worms which seems safer to be left locked up deep within.

Over the next couple of days, just allow to float back into your memory those little instances when you have encountered that strange sensation of somehow knowing something without understanding why, of feeling yourself suddenly connected to some wonderful, inexplicable energy which briefly flitted in and out of your being. I know that a whole host of such instances offered themselves to me before a confrontation with my own mortality finally shoved that inner truth right under my nose, so that I could no longer run away from it.

Once I could no longer escape it, that inner reality became firmly planted into my whole being to the extent that it is my guiding energy, the fundamental force within my life which I now trust to create my outer reality. It now seems to me amazing that I denied this part of me for so long, yet I have come to understand more and more that we each of us have our own pace and our own time to grow. It is irrelevant whether one person seems to 'get their act together' faster than another, as time itself does not truly exist: it too is a product of the rational mind which sees everything in finite terms.

There are those of us who are only now becoming aware of this other dimension; there are others who seem to have been on the 'spiritual path' for ever but who always seem to be banging our heads on something which bogs us down and weakens our resolve and faith; there are yet others for whom life seems to be speeding along but within whom there is still a sense of 'not doing enough'.

All of this does not matter. The important thing is that we are always *aware* – aware that change is always occurring within us, aware of our hearts and our intuition, aware that we are not alone in this quest for our own inner completion. For there are now so many on this path, creating an energy which now cannot be rolled back, not only in our own lives but in the life of this planet. Do not compare yourself with others; what matters at this time is what is going on within yourself.

And if you really need to get in touch with that Healer Within, you must first learn to trust it and yourself. Some obstacles may seem too heavy to bear, but remember that the greater the obstacle, the greater the inner challenge. We would not still be in this physical form if we had completed what we have come here to fulfil.

25

When we lie in bed and are sick and filled with pain, there is that sense of being trapped within our bodies, unable to escape the realm of physical sensation. I am sure we all know the feeling only too well.

This feeling is the extreme of what it means to be within our physical bodies. In this physical world into which we choose to enter, we are literally trapped within our bodies. We are bombarded by a whole host of sensations, some pleasurable, some painful, but, for sure, we are unable to run away from and leave our bodies when we see something unpleasant coming towards us. Within this tiny vehicle which is our physical form, we have to stand and face everything which comes to us. It is within the constraints of this physical form that the most profound change and growth occurs to that eternal part of us, our spirit, which is conected to the Whole. As we expand and evolve, so it is that we contribute to the expansion and evolution of the Universe as an entity unto itself.

When our spirit makes its transition through death from the physical to the ethereal realm, there is always a period, immeasurable by our own time, when we are in a state of limbo between the two. This is an active state during which we integrate into our inner being all of the profound experiences and growth which we underwent in our physical form. We literally see our whole lifetime pass in front of us and feel and understand all that this has to teach us: not just what we experienced in our own lives, but also the energy we put out which created an impact in the lives of others.

This is, in a sense, where the notion of heaven and hell comes from, as we must go through the sensation of what it was like to be at the receiving end of our own actions, as well as understanding the emotions and feelings we assumed from others. If we were intentionally cruel to others, then the sensation of that pain would pass through our own spirit in order to be understood and released; if our actions were guided by a gentle, unconditional love, we feel and understand and then release this sensation in a similar manner.

This heaven and hell is not the great 'judgment' of traditional christianity where we are doomed to one state or the other for eternity; it is the final period of growth which began with our physical birth. It is a short, intense burst of learning the final lessons of a lifetime, before we join the true Light of the Whole and continue with our evolution.

I have on a number of occasions sat with people as they are making that transition into death and I learned very quickly that a person can hear and take in the energy of our being and words even when he or she seems to be unconscious or incoherent. Most of us will at some point in our lives have to go through this experience with a dear one and putting out an energy and words of love and forgiveness creates a vibration around the physical form which opens the door for an easy transition into a higher plane. The power of unconditional love is so great that it sweeps away, at this stage, any pain and fear which our loved one may still be holding on to. This is so important to recognize, because someone who is dying will hold on to life and even physical pain much longer than he has to, if he is unable to let go of the memory of suffering and any unresolved fear that death will bring a continuation of such suffering.

This is why I have dedicated this book to nurses, because they do this every day with their selfless love, often without fully understanding the extent of what they do.

It may seem a little strange to you that I am writing so much about death so early on in a book about healing.

The reason I am doing so is to try to take away the fear of it which can so easily paralyze someone faced with their own mortality and to confront the resignation that many people feel about the limited nature of their lives. I also wish, at this point, to shed some light on the connection which exists between our physical life on earth and the realm into which we enter after the death of our physical bodies.

The Central American Indians say: 'Life is but a dream. Only when we die do we wake up!' And, indeed, in a certain way, this physical life of ours on Earth is an illusion, as it is only a small part of our existence, while appearing to us as the whole. We only begin to see how big the real picture is when we pass over to the 'other side' and truly become aware of being an integral part of the whole.

There are many who have experienced or at least felt some kind of contact with someone who has passed over to the other side. Even if we have not consciously felt that contact, it is established in our sleeping hours when our conscious and subconscious worlds are brought into alignment with each other.

There are certain beings with whom we have a very special bond, both in this world and beyond. Throughout our earthly existence, we are continuously meeting people and, once in a blue moon, we meet someone whom we feel we have known forever after only having spoken to him or her for a few minutes. These are those special people with whom we can always be our true selves and with whom we can always pick up where we left off even if we see each other rarely.

These are people with whom we have gone through many lifetimes together and who always stimulate us, just as we do to them, to grow and to learn more quickly. Likewise, there are many beings who are not presently in physical form and with whom there is an equally special bond; they are those who have chosen to work with us from the other side in ways which we obviously find difficult to understand in a rational sense. These may included people, such as close family and friends, who have died in our lifetime, but those who have the strongest connection with us are those – it may be even just one – who have been working with us since our birth: what people variously call our guides, helpers etc..

The purpose of this connection, in particular in this era of immense change, is to act as an intermediary between the total life force of the Whole and our individual spirit as a part of this Whole. As we grow and learn and get closer to our true essence, we are 'fed' with more knowledge and 'supplied' with new challenges to stimulate this growth even further. For, within this Universe of intricate connections, there is no chance. Everything which we encounter in our lives is there for some reason, however obscure it may feel to be, and the way we *choose* to react to it determines what other choices will be subsequently laid before us. This is no almighty power which predetermines the way our lives turn out to be; we have free will to chart our own course, and even if, in retrospect, we sometimes feel we have made the wrong choice, we are always offered other choices to guide us back on a similar path.

These 'guides' may work with us in different aspects of our lives, from our own personal growth to the effect that we will have on individuals or the society around us or even the vibration of our planet as a whole. But, because the idea of such a connection with non-physical beings is dismissed by our rationally based system of 'knowledge', we do not draw upon such guidance as much as we really can. Most of us do not set aside time in our day to day lives to sit in stillness and open ourselves up to that 'still, small voice'.

Even fewer of us, when in crisis, will open ourselves up in faith and ask for guidance, for an understanding of what we are to learn from the crisis. When we ask for help from a source outside ourselves, we must be prepared for an answer which will require action from ourselves rather than passively praying for an outside power to just put everything right for us. If we open ourselves up to the knowledge and guidance of God and the Universe, then we can help ourselves. We are ultimately the only ones who have the power to create transformation in our lives.

If I am ever in a state of crisis, I will usually, before I go to bed, close my eyes and pray to my guides to feed me with the knowledge which will enable me to learn from and overcome the crisis by my own thoughts and actions. It is something I only do in the rare times of real crisis, as overuse of such contact for less important matters tends to dilute the energy coming through, and I generally find that, overnight or during the course of the following day, the message will come through – most often in the most unexpected and oblique way.

In reading about these guides and helpers, we may imagine them to be wonderful angelic beings who seem so different from ourselves. But, in this continual cycle of life, it only happens to be at this point in our perception of time that they are giving such love and attention to us; we have done exactly the same to them and others at other times. At present, we are in 'mortal flesh', but when we die and leave this physical form behind, we enter into another plane of existence and may choose to be 'there' for others with whom we share a close bond.

That is why it is so important not to view death as a failure. In this current AIDS epidemic, I have worked with many who have died seemingly before their time, and I have recently, in my meditation, begun to feel their collective spirit coming through me very strongly. I have no doubt that they are working at this moment not only with many individuals still on this planet, but also for a greater transformation within humanity as a whole which we cannot even begin to understand.

In this whole cycle, it is important to recognize that we are the ones who are at this moment trapped within our bodies and therefore forced to face our own change and evolution. As they help us from the lightness of their existence, so we shall do for them some day. Even now, they themselves learn through our experience.

All we have to do is trust that bond.

Children and Parents

When I was a young child, I had three 'imaginary friends': Mockey, Vinegar and Louise Fishwater!

I do not actually remember having these friends, but, when my parents told me at about the age of seven that I had had them, I decided to kill them off, as the idea was really rather childish for a boy of seven! Louise Fishwater drowned; Vinegar died of exposure in the Swiss Alps; maybe I generously left Mockey wandering around somewhere!

It is only in recent years that I have re-established contact with these friends, my guides. Each of them has a very distinct energy when they come through to me and each works with me on a different level of my existence and growth.

However, I do not intend to give you a detailed description of Mockey, Vinegar and Louise Fishwater! Such childhood, imaginary friends are of course not uncommon and I bring them up, because their appearance in my life, and subsequent disappearance and reappearance, reflect what goes on within a child during its formative years, in particular the first seven.

When a child is born, that special individual essence, its spirit, is by no means yet fully there within its tiny body. The young infant has a certain sensory perception of what is going on around it, yet there are those familiar times when it appears to go off into a different world. As it grows older, the child begins to relate more strongly to its environment, especially its nurturing parents. Everyone who is a parent for the first time goes through the delight of discovering each miniscule change in reaction as the baby opens new horizons.

In a sense, the various stages of development in a child mirror stages of development in humanity. Just as mankind in its early stages of evolution had not developed a consciousness of separateness, so a child originally sees the world as a blurred reality in which everything merges together. Its five senses are not yet as distinct and refined as in later life, and there is still a connection with the wholeness of the Universe which is lost as the child grows older. Hence, the 'imaginary friends' are just as much part of the child's world as the 'real' people around it.

A child is not just born and instantly becomes a mini human being. The spirit of the new being does not enter into the physical foetus in the womb until the contract is fully made on a deep level between the parent and the being. Sometimes, in the case of abortion and even miscarriage, the parent is not ready for the child to be born or, in some cases, a lesson has to be learned by the parent through the abortion or miscarriage; in these cases, the new being that is to incarnate as the child has not fully entered into the physical form and therefore neither abortion nor a miscarriage necessarily mean the destruction of a life in the most complete sense.

During the first seven years of life, the essential spirit of the child enters more and more into its body until finally the child reaches the stage of being able to formulate such abstract concepts as 'What would happen if . . .?', and becomes more strongly aware of itself as a separate individual in its own right. This is the point that the rational mind has really begun to take hold, and comparison and competition become key components of a child's behavior. It is also at this point that the new being or child is fully within the physical world as we know it as adults.

Before the age of seven, the child is still tied very much to the mother's or nurturing parent's apron strings – indeed, in etheric terms, there is a very real cord which binds mother and child together. This bond is very important because a child, during this period, is still working on a level where it has a foot in the non-physical world from where it has come. The bond with the nurturing parent is the grounding cord in a physical sense which counteracts all the energy that is being poured into the child from the spiritual plane. This energy is fundamentally a gradual transfer of the individual essence of the new child from the higher vibration of the spiritual plane to the lower level of vibration on a physical plane. If this was transfered all in one go at the birth of the child, it would literally blast the physical body apart.

This is why the first seven years of a child's life are so vital. If that connection between the child and the nurturing parent is broken or disrupted during this time, whether through death or a disharmonious atmosphere in the home, the effect can be for the child to spin off on a level where it temporarily loses real touch with its physical reality. This is what is often meant by a 'spacey' kid – one who does not have the grounding force to counteract the higher energy which is the source of his intelligence and intuitive perceptions. Much, for example, has been written about children of alcoholics: for them, the traumas they experience and the patterns of behavior they pick up from their parents begin with this lack of tangible connection and grounding they receive in these early years.

During this period, therefore, physical contact and affection are of utmost importance, preferably from both parents. A baby will tell you soon enough when it has had enough and needs to go to sleep: sleep being the time when that process of transition from energy of the spirit to energy of the earth takes place.

Almost as important is the understanding that a child, from the moment it is born and even earlier, is a sentient being who picks up on every vibration around it. Although it may not at an early age have the rational capacity to understand language, it reacts to and absorbs the tonality of words. The relationship between parents and child will build on a vibrational level and will be clearly inset within the child's psyche long before true verbal communication takes place.

Parents will come up again and again in the practical section of this book, and it is for this reason that I am dwelling on the relationship between parent and child upon the broader, spiritual plane.

Probably, one of the most difficult concepts for people to grasp or accept in this book is the idea that *we all choose our parents*. It is also one of the most important ones for us to understand, for, in doing so, we are able to see before us a whole new way of relating to our parents, especially if there are major problems and obstacles in this relationship.

Without question, parents are the strongest formative influence on our lives. Their influence remains with us long after we have left home or even after they have died. In our early childhood, we accept everything we hear from them; then, gradually, we grow to question until we reach that stage of rebellion where we must assert our own sense of independence if this is not granted to us. Some children are blessed with a loving, open relationship with their parents as they grow older; others become completely alienated; the majority of us, though, find ourselves somewhere in between, where things have to be resolved on various levels.

So, when I say that we choose our parents, what do I mean?

In the cycle of life, as we pass through a multitude of incarnations, we build up a mountain of relationships with those people we meet. In essence, relationships are the forming structure of our lives, as it is through contact with others that we change and evolve.

When our physical body dies, the relationships of this lifetime do not die with it; their substance remains and carries through into the new plane of reality. In many cases, relationships are not resolved and are carried forward to continue in another lifetime or sphere. (This is the basis of what is called 'karma' in the East). Relationships are only ever fully resolved when a perfect balance between two beings is reached: i.e. where there exists the harmonious flow of unconditional giving and receiving of love which I will discuss in the later chapters on love and relationships.

Our parents are usually those with whom we have shared many lifetimes together and with whom there is generally much unresolved 'business'. But, it is not just for this reason that we choose them as our parents.

Those of us who have had more than our fair share of conflict with our parents are often those who have carved our own path in our lives. When we come into opposition with our parents on some fundamental issue or over a whole sequence of events, we are brought face to face with the reality of calling into question those symbols and values which our parents represent for us. This in turn brings us to the point of re-evaluating all our own thoughts and actions, so that we are forced to rely on our own conscience and heart to guide us, rather than accept the ideology which has been handed down to us.

There is no doubt that such conflict causes pain on all sides, especially if this continues unabated without there seeming to be any point where the two sides will meet in the middle. And yet, in undergoing the intensity of this experience, the consciousness of the child is stimulated towards a greater level of growth than would have occurred within the framework of a more harmonious relationship.

If you have had a life of such conflict with your family, just for a moment look within yourself and see how this has given to you an extra dimension, a deeper insight into your own true essence as well as a greater understanding of and compassion for the plight of others.

And when you see this, bless your parents, for they too have gone through their pain. While your pain has led you to a deeper perception of yourself and of others, theirs, as parents, has led them to, and may still be leading them to, the ultimate lesson of letting go, of not trying to control, of trusting. As you progress through this book, you will see how all paths lead ultimately to this process of letting go and learning faith; going through this process with your child and learning to accept your children as they are, rather than seeing them as an extension of yourself, can be one of the most painful lessons that anyone can be taught.

And so, let me return to the question of choosing our parents. Before we choose to incarnate in a physical form, we choose to enter into an environment which is going to stimulate us towards the appropriate potential for growth. Our parents are the most vital ingredient of this environment and we therefore enter into a kind of mutual contract with them. They too are part of this decision, on a level of their higher selves of which their physical selves are not aware, for the growth that they experience is also part of the relationship. Sometimes, it will take lifetimes for balance and harmony to be restored in the relationship.

The reason I have gone into this rather involved explanation of this complex interrelationship is that most people I have encountered who are going through periods of painful struggle and change are, whatever age they may be, carrying around with them a lot of unresolved excess baggage in relation to their parents. (This is nothing new: any psychiatrist will tell you the same.)

Children can be very unforgiving, because we take so personally everything that our parents lay upon us, without stopping to think that they too had parents and probably went through similar conflicts themselves. This interrelationship between parent and child is a primeval force which shapes the growth of an individual and, in a collective sense, society as a whole.

The pace of change has now increased in our world to such an extent that the difference and, therefore, conflict between parent and child has grown with each generation. We have, in many ways, inherited the accumulated experience and conflict which has been handed down from generation to generation in our individual families.

If we are able to release and let go of the conflict by forgiving our parents, loving them as they are and not judging them, then we will be in a greater position of strength to pass this understanding and unconditional love on to our own children. If we hold on to any pain related to our family, it is likely that this will at some point be manifested in our relationship with our own children, so that we must go through the lesson of forgiveness all over again.

If this very basic conflict were released within the confines of each individual family, just imagine the effect it would have on the balance and harmony within our world as a whole.

The Physical and the Spiritual

All that I have written in the last two chapters may seem somewhat deep and metaphysical without having a great deal to do with whatever it is that you wish to heal in your life. I may appear to have given the impression that there is a great distinction between the physical and spiritual, but they are in reality one and the same thing.

The spiritual is the eternal, the part of us which continues for ever; the physical is the temporal, what we experience in this earthly existence. Since we are at this moment in our physical bodies on earth, the spiritual and physical combine together and the fulfillment and ease of our day to day lives is very much determined by the extent to which we can bring these two seeming opposites into unity.

The spiritual is the higher vibration; the physical is the denser energy. Therefore, the physical comes at the end of the chain: what is occurring on the spiritual, ethereal, mental and emotional planes will finally manifest on the physical plane. If we are in a state of balance within the realms of the spirit, mind and emotions, this will be mirrored in our physical state. There are very few on this planet who are in perfect balance and harmony, so nearly all of us are at some point prone to colds, aches and pains. Then, there are others who are in an extreme state of imbalance and disharmony on the subtler planes, and this will gradually filter down to the physical body, making them vulnerable to all sorts of viruses or foreign organisms which our immune system would normally fight off.

This does *not* mean to say – and I wish to stress this – that the one whose body is unbalanced is inferior to the one who is in a state of inner harmony. It also does not mean that someone who is sick is at fault. This sickness is merely to serve as a pointer that all is not in balance on other planes. Likewise, someone whose life is filled with emotional drama and turmoil is getting a similar message: that this is a reflection of the state of disharmony on the mental and ethereal planes.

Maybe I should at this time stop and explain what I mean by these various levels.

The ethereal plane is that level of vibration at which our higher self and physical self are linked. Although part of the same reality, the physical self is generally not aware of the plane of the higher self, as it is only in our dreams or in deep meditation that our experiences on the physical plane are fully absorbed and worked out on the higher vibration. As mentioned in the previous chapter, the unity between these two selves still exists to a certain extent within the being of an infant; its rational capabilities are not sufficiently developed to create a distinction between them.

This is why sleep is necessary for us. If we did not sleep, not only would our bodily functions be impaired, but also the work which we are doing on a spiritual plane would quite literally drive us out of our minds. When we sleep, all the levels of our being, from the spiritual to the physical, are integrated: our physical, emotional and mental experience is passed up to the higher vibration which sees the larger picture and, simultaneously, subliminal messages are passed down to the denser levels of vibration.

If it always seems to be that you need more sleep than most people, this may well be that you are at present going through a lot of inner transformation which needs time to be absorbed into all levels of your being. Many politicians and 'workaholics' need less sleep because their energy is always being directed towards the outer world rather than the inner world of personal growth. (It is, by the way, the inner change of masses of individuals which ultimately transform the world; our politicians are, though they do not understand this, merely a reflection of the people they 'serve'!)

If you are going through a particularly intense period of growth or suffering, it is not a bad idea to keep a pad beside your bed and write down your dreams as soon as you wake up. Otherwise, you tend to forget them, which is no problem, as they have still registered in your subconscious. But, the message will come through more easily if your conscious mind and subconscious are working at the same time.

It is along the ethereal level, therefore, that the path for our highest potential and rate of growth is determined, as this is the plane on which we are connected to the Whole which we call God or the Universe. If there is, within our physical lives, any major, long-term deviation from the path of our highest fulfillment and potential, a chain reaction begins from the ethereal plane downwards which may ultimately manifest on the physical plane as a dis-ease, in order to make us look more deeply into the inner direction of our lives.

The mental plane is the level on which we receive the primary 'message' from the ethereal plane. If we are open and clear on this level, we receive this 'message' as an intuitive thought upon which we immediately act. This is the point of will and decision to create our reality. It is also the point at which the reactions of our emotions and sense perceptions are processed up to the ethereal plane and related to the path of least resistance which is our highest good.

Our emotions are the link between our mental processes and our physical reality. They govern the human relationships which dominate our lives. We often get stuck on this plane by holding on to the emotional charge caused by close contact with the energy of another being, rather than understanding and nurturing the essential lightness and freedom of our spirit; we confuse what is really our true essence with

40

the excess baggage which we subconsciously take on from others.

The physical plane, being the densest, is the level on which we experience the result of all that we do, think or feel. Thus, through all the challenges which we are forced to confront, it is the plane on which we have the most continuous potential for growth. It is the receptive plane in that the nature of these challenges are determined by our higher self which is connected to the Whole, the Universe or God – (or, as some people would view it, Chance – a concept which does not exist in a Universe of infinite, intricate connections).

The physical plane is also the beginning of the return cycle up to the ethereal planes. In this upward cycle, our sense perceptions and experiences on this physical plane are passed through to the emotional plane which reacts to them; they are then pushed upwards to our mental plane which refines them, so that, on the ethereal and spiritual level, our higher self, which is connected to that Universal Whole, will learn and grow and expand. If any of these stages on this cycle are disrupted, blockages appear which will ultimately be imprinted on the ethereal level (or our aura), finally reappearing again in our lower vibrational levels as some form of emotional or physical imbalance.

So it is that health, whether on a physical, emotional or mental level, is balance, while dis-ease is imbalance. It is as simple as that. But, unfortunately for us, what causes the imbalance is never simple – certainly not to us, who are always too much on top of it to see the cause clearly.

For me, this usually manifests itself as a cold or, for specific blockages I have learned to recognize, slight aches in certain parts of my body. These usually disappear almost as soon as I understand and release the cause of the blockage, a process which can take from minutes to weeks! Greater imbalances such as spraining my ankle or passing a kidney stone come to me when I really *must* confront and release a particular aspect of my physical existence which is blocking my inner growth.

And, so it is for all of us. Throughout our lives, we get little nudges to keep us on course. But, then, we may all of a sudden be confronted with something, whether a physical disease or accident or emotional trauma, which we cannot turn away from.

This is when we have to start looking deeper within ourselves.

The Endocrine System

Finally, it is time to relate all this talk of balance and disharmony, health and dis-ease to our physical bodies.

First of all, I wish to put what we call physical diseases into perspective. Most are caused by microscopic organisms such as viruses or bacteria. They have evolved into highly efficient organisms, latching on to a source of life whenever the opportunity is presented.

Yet, it is important to understand that, of all living organisms on this planet, man is the most highly evolved, while a virus is one of the simplest forms of life on earth. The bodily systems within man, in particular the immune system, are equipped to destroy any hostile intruder and do so when they are in one hundred percent working order.

It is only when there is a state of imbalance within our bodies that these highly efficient systems begin to fail us. Homeostasis is the medical term used for the intricate balance that is maintained within our physical bodies. From the simplest physical reactions to the most complex thoughts, it is the co-operation between the millions of miscroscopic cells within us that keeps us functioning throughout every second of our earthly existence – just as a beehive cannot survive without the unified purpose of all its members.

The two primary systems which are responsible for maintaining this homeostasis are our nervous and endocrine systems. It is on these which I now wish to focus.

Just close your eyes for a moment and concentrate on that very central part of yourself which runs from your brain down to the very base of your back – this is of course your spine and wrapped around it is your central nervous system.

There are three kinds of nerves, all of which are connected to the brain through the spinal cord: the sensory nerves which bring our sensory perceptions into the brain; the motor nerves which send signals from the brain to our limbs etc.; and the autonomic nervous system which maintains regular nervous functions such as the beating of the heart. All three are essential to the maintenance of balance within the body by instantly sending messages between the brain and any part of the body which is threatened by imbalance.

The endocrine system works in tandem with the nervous system and, by the particular way it works, is the most essential system for maintaining balance or homeostasis in the body over the long term.

Unlike the nervous system which sends messages rapidly to its target organs, the endocrine system works by a much more slow moving process. It operates through chemical messengers or hormones which circulate in the blood and modify the activity of the various vital organs throughout our bodies. It is a change in the body's internal or external environment which initially triggers the release of these hormones into the bloodstream; once balance has been restored, a process called 'biofeedback' occurs, whereby this balance is conveyed back to the initial point of control and the secretion of the hormones ceases.

Hormones are stored in and released from the endocrine glands and it is on the ones relevant to this book which I shall now focus, not just in a purely physiological sense, but their effect on the broader aspects of balance within us.

The pineal and pituitary glands: The pituitary gland is known as the 'master gland', as its activity controls many of the other glands beneath it in the body. It is linked, through the hypothalamus, to the brain and thereby to the central nervous system.

Virtually nothing is yet known by modern science about the pineal gland, which is situated in the brain above the pituitary gland. In fact, the pineal gland is the 'inspiration' of the endocrine system, transmitting many messages to the rest of the body, sometimes through the pituitary gland, sometimes by-passing it.

The Thyroid and parathyroid glands are located in the throat; they are responsible for metabolism and the regulation of our physical and mental growth.

The sex glands – the testes in men and ovaries in women. Aside from their obvious reproductive function, they also have considerable influence on those less physical aspects of us which we call our moods and emotions.

The Thymus and the Heart Center

It is very sad how the thymus gland is so very much misunderstood and so totally underestimated. If there is one part of this chapter that I wish you to firmly implant into your mind, it is this one, as I shall be referring again and again to this section of the body and, in particular, what it represents on a level that has implications far beyond the purely physical.

If you read any text book on physiology, this vital organ will be given barely a paragraph. It is known that this is where the T-cells mature within the unborn baby and also that it shrinks as a child reaches puberty. Because it becomes smaller at this age, it has long been presumed that it no longer has any real function in the human body after adolescence.

They could not be more mistaken. You only have to look at the size of the thymus in a body of a person who has died of AIDS to fully understand how shrunken the thymus can become when a person's immune system has been totally wrecked.

In a healthy adult, however small it may be compared with pre-adolescence, the thymus gland, in association with its neighbor the heart, is *the regulating system of the whole immune system*.

45

It will only be a matter of years before scientists fully discover the extent of this, and, indeed, discoveries are already being made to point in this direction. (An excellent book which established this in a scientific, empirical manner is coincidentally also entitled *The Healer Within*, published by E.P. Dutton, New York.)

The thymus lies at a point level with the heart, roughly where the heart would be if it were centrally located. It is at the focal point of the Heart Center, about which you will be reading much more later on.

The heart is, as we all know, associated with love, and how many of us have heard the old saying: 'Love heals'?

The Adrenal Glands and Stress
I'm going to start this section off with a story.

Imagine that you are a stone-age man walking along by yourself and you suddenly come face to face with a sabre-tooth tiger. You freeze and in an instant make the decision whether to flee or stand and fight. The outcome is simple: either you escape or kill the tiger or you end up as a tasty meal.

This in a basic way illustrates what is called the 'Flight or Fight Syndrome', which is closely linked to our adrenal glands. When we are confronted with something like the sabre-tooth tiger or, in other words, when our brain receives the signal that there is some outer threat to ourselves, our adrenal glands, which lie perched on top of our kidneys, secrete certain hormones which direct most of our energy to the outer limits of our body, our limbs. This is done in association with messages sent from the brain to the motor nervous system. When the threat is past, normal balance is restored through biofeedback.

The 'Flight or Fight Syndrome' is also associated with that vague concept we call stress.

Stress, in a physiological sense, is exactly what it says. If you build a footbridge, the iron girders with which it is built are chosen because they are strong enough to carry the anticipated weight load of the bridge indefinitely. If, however, it was suddenly decided that this bridge would be used by cars and trucks, then the stress on these girders would be greater than what they were built for and one of them would finally give way, leading to the collapse of the whole structure.

Well, stress within the body is no different. The human body is built to live in a reasonably stable environment with emergency systems built in to react against periodic shocks from outside. In the case of the sabre-tooth tiger, or, for that matter, a 400-metre sprint, the body increases its output of energy. When it is over, the body slowly returns to normal.

So-called 'emotional stress', on the other hand, is a completely different matter. Most of us in the West are fortunate enough to be living in a society in which physical threats to our lives are rare. Yet, such is the way that 'civilized' man has developed that he has allowed other factors to impinge upon his life and upon the emotional stability of his being. Some of these, such as the death of a spouse or relative, are at some time in our lives inevitable, but there are of course many other causes of stress.

Whether stemming from work, relationships or whatever, the physiological result is the same. Any emotional reaction has an immediate effect on the body – a simple example is of an angry man who goes red in the face – yet, as in the case of the sabre-tooth tiger, a short-term emotional outburst does not necessarily do any harm to the body. After the fact, the body returns to normal.

How many of us, though, are the type who express emotion and, in doing so, immediately release it? Very few, I suspect, and it is this inability to let go of an emotional experience which causes most damage to our bodies.

Let us return to the girder again. If, for instance, just one car is allowed over the bridge, it may groan and bend, but, once the car has passed over, the bridge will be in no immediate danger of collapsing. If, on the other hand, cars will continue to cross the bridge *ad infinitum*, the weight of each car will have an accumulative effect on the girder until it can finally take no more and collapses.

The human body is of course an infinitely more complex organism than an iron girder, but the same process occurs with long-term stress within a human being. When there is an element of emotional stress within a person's life, the brain perceives it in the same way as it perceives any threat to the entity which it controls, and sends out messages to counter any effect it has upon the body. As with physical stress, it is the endocrine system, and the adrenal glands in particular, which do most of the work, secreting hormones to deal with any imbalance that may have occurred on a cellular level.

However, there is a fundamental difference between the working and effect of physical and emotional or mental stress. Whereas physical stress is almost always relatively short-term and can be identified through the nervous system as coming from a specific location, non-physical stress can be carried around unresolved for huge stretches of time and cannot be identified as coming from a specific physical location.

So, what happens when we carry unresolved stress around with us is quite simply that our body is searching for something it cannot specifically react to and is therefore always on red alert, using energy for nothing. Or, more to the point, the natural balance within the body, homeostasis, is disturbed and all the major functions which maintain health within the body are impaired. And of course the immune system is one of these.

Although I have used the word stress throughout this chapter, it is really too general a term. Just as I have explained its effect on the body in a very basic, simplified manner, I have used the word stress to cover a whole host of influences on our lives. Throughout our lives, there are things that happen to us which cause us suffering – some of us put the suffering behind us, accepting that this is a part of life, a means of learning and growing; others, indeed most of us at some point in our lives, hold on to the emotion behind the experience and allow this to fester within us, often quite subconsciously. Many of us will continuously carry around with us worries about work or a relationship, but there are far deeper rooted emotions and experiences which we carry around with us and of which, in our day to day lives, we are not consciously aware.

The bulk and most important part of this book focuses on the identification, understanding and, finally, release of these elements within us which I have described here as stress and which are the primary causes of imbalance taking root within our bodies.

The Seven Chakras

The reasons I have focused so strongly on the endocrine system are twofold, both interconnected. Firstly, there is the physiological function of maintaining balance within the body. Secondly, and of equal importance, these physical glands are directly linked to the Chakras – non-physical 'energy centers' which are every bit as real as the endocrine system, although few can see them on the physical plane.

Although they are others, there are seven principal Chakras, which form a major link between the physical and ethereal planes. When an individual comes to see me for a treatment, I will generally work on that person's chakras.

Each healer works in his or her way. Many will be drawn to the parts of the body which are causing problems, but, for whatever reason, my mind never focuses on the physical body. What comes to me, both before and while I am working with the chakras, are the inner sources of imbalance within an individual which cause the outer problem to occur. Whether they are emotional, psychological or even deeper, I feel and see in my mind's eye what it is that is holding people back from creating harmony within their lives and what are the major changes they need to make in their thought patterns, their actions and their relationships with other people. It is through this experience and my own inner experiences that I have come to write this and other books.

Before I move on to the chakras in more detail, I wish

to write something briefly about healing for those of you who feel that you would like to go out and be a 'healer'. The first advice I have is to forget such labels as being a 'healer'. We all have healing powers within us and we use them on a day to day basis much more than we understand, especially when our hearts are open. If people are healers, it is because they do not see this energy as coming from themselves; they open themselves to be a channel for that life force, which is the Universe. It is as simple as that.

Secondly, if you feel that 'healing power' within you, it may well be that you will study courses on one or more specific branches of healing, of which there are, of course, many. The main object of this is to give you confidence and to give you a specific tool to work with.

My strong advice, though, is this. Use a particular process until it becomes second nature to you. Then, start to leave the teachings of others behind and just follow your own intuition. You will never reach your fullest potential as a healer when you are still focusing on the details of what you have been taught. Only when you start to trust the guidance of your own inner voice and do what *feels* right to you – only then do you let yourself get out of the way and allow the Energy really to flow.

And, of course, the same applies to the process of healing yourself.

As we shall be working together on the chakras in the practical section of this book, it would do no harm to visualize these energy centers.

As I asked you to do earlier when writing about the central nervous system, just close your eyes for a few moments and focus on that central part of yourself which is your spinal cord running from your brain down to the base of your spine where you sit down. It is along your spine that your chakras are situated, the first pointing downwards, the seventh upwards and the five in between out in front of you.

In order to visualize them, see in your mind's eye the shape of a cone, or, more specifically, a swirling energy

in the shape of a whirlpool or the eye of a tornado, with
the narrowest point fixed in the spinal cord and the widest
point coming about two inches out from the body. It does
not matter if you find it difficult to visualize in this way. The
important thing is to have a frame of reference and to sense
them as being points of energy within you, continuously in
motion.

The notion of chakras has mainly been passed on to us
from the religions of the East, although they are also part
of the Western Mystery School tradition which has been
hidden from us for so long and is only now beginning to
reappear.

To certain Buddhist or Hindu purists, my interpreta-
tion of the chakras may sometimes seem to stray from
the 'accepted wisdom'. I see two reasons for this. One is
that Western man is in many ways very different from his
Eastern cousin and has a distinct psychology – (the importance of ego and competition in the Western world is one of
the cornerstones of this distinction). Secondly, we as human
beings are changing and evolving at such a rapid rate that
many old distinctions disappear and new ones appear in their
place. All the chakras are, to a certain extent, interdependent
and I find the boundaries between certain of them to be less
rigid than I was first led to believe.

The First Chakra is situated at that very point at the base of the
spine where you sit down, called the coccyx bone. Pointing
downwards from here, it is our connection to the earth, our
basic instinct for survival, our 'common sense'. It is at this
point that the immense energy of the earth enters into our
being and spirals up through the other chakras to reach the
ethereal plane. This is also the source of our sexual energy,
the power of which, ask we will see later, should never be
underestimated. (This chakra, as well as the second chakra,
is connected to our sex glands). Finally, it is also through
here that there is a special connection between a child and
its nurturing parent.

The Second Chakra is centered two finger widths below

the navel and points outwards in front of the body. It is the seat of SEXUALITY, EMOTIONS, CREATIVITY and, as it happens, psychic capabilities. It is connected to the sex glands within the endocrine system.

The Third Chakra is located in the solar plexus, just below the breastbone. It is the center of POWER and STRENGTH, EGO and FAITH. These may seem vague terms, but this chakra is the most vital in the current evolution of Western man – and also the most difficult to understand and to bring into balance. It is connected to the adrenal glands, as is, to a certain degree, the second.

The Fourth Chakra is on the level of the heart, but, unlike the physical position of the heart, is along the central line down which the spinal cord runs. It is often called the Gateway to Heaven, as this marks the beginning of the 'higher' aspects of man. It is the center of LOVE and COMPASSION and is connected to the thymus gland.

The Fifth Chakra is located in the throat and is the center of COMMUNICATION and EXPRESSION. Because creativity and emotions have much to do with this center, there is a strong link between this and the second chakra. In addition to this primary chakra, there are subsidiary chakras attached to it which are in the hands, particularly the palms and the fingertips. This chakra is linked to the thyroid and parathyroid glands.

The Sixth Chakra is the renowned Third Eye just above the eyebrows. Here is the seat of our INTUITION and CLAIRVOYANCE, as well as the RATIONAL MIND. It is connected to the pituitary gland.

The Seventh Chakra is at the top of our head, our Crown, and points upwards. It is our direct, personal link to our higher self, and thus to the Whole which we call the Universe or God. It is our ultimate guiding force and brings all the other six chakras together as one. It is connected to the pineal gland.

The Chakras and
Our Physical Anatomy

I write this final chapter of 'Understanding the Healer Within' with a certain amount of reluctance.

I have already explained how the incidence of disease in our lives is a vehicle for change, often in the broadest sense. There are certain diseases, though, which are associated with fairly specific causes of imbalance deep within us, and relating certain parts of our anatomy to certain of our chakras is the focus of this chapter.

I say that I write this with some reluctance, as these are meant only to be very rough guidelines, rather than me telling you specifically that you came down with a certain disease because you were dealing with a particular aspect of your life in the wrong way. I have read certain books which explain sickness in these very narrow terms, and they do not feel right to me.

As you go through the practical section of this book, you will see that every one of us has various degrees of imbalance within us, but this is not attributable to just one source. The root causes of imbalance are many, and they are always inextricably related in a very complex manner.

Therefore, when you read through these guidelines, I ask you to accept them as, at best, a means of taking your focus away from the physical side of disease, so that you may concentrate on your inner growth.

The First and Second Chakras

What first comes to mind with these chakras are diseases related to the sexual organs, and there is certainly a frequent correlation between these physical organs and what sex means on an emotional and psychological level. Most often, any imbalance within the male and female reproductive organs, including the prostate in younger men, is associated with an unsatisfactory *depth* of sexual contact, or else feelings of guilt or uncleanliness with regard to one's sexuality.

Also associated with these lower chakras are the releasing areas of the rectum, bladder, lower intestines and the descending colon – and, on an emotional plane, releasing is exactly what they do represent, a lack of which can cause imbalance within this area.

The Third Chakra

This is definitely the most important section. As you will see later in the practical section of the book, it is within the second and third chakra that the greatest imbalance occurs, and the two are closely related in the way that we control and suppress (third chakra) our emotions (second chakra) instead of releasing them.

The liver is our most important organ after our heart and brain, in that it is the processing plant for almost all the body's substances. Its proper function is dependent on it remaining a clear channel, and many results of addictive behavior, in particular excess drugs and alcohol, have a very damaging effect on it.

Imbalance and disease within the liver nearly always mean a deep imbalance within the third chakra, in particular when the issue is control: usually a need to control, hiding a fear of losing control. Associated with this is a lack of trust in who you are: feeling in one way, but acting out in another; putting a mask over your true self.

The same applies to the gall bladder, and pain in the middle of one's back, on a level with the third chakra, will also often be related to an unwillingness to accept oneself as

55

one is, sometimes manifesting itself as guilt.

Imbalance within the stomach, such as indigestion and ulcers, is also connected to control, in particular impatience, intolerance and an ability to deal with authority. In severe conditions, such as cancer and severe ulcers, this can be brought about by the stoic refusal to express anger or resentment.

The pancreas is most often associated with the disease of diabetes and is also a subsidiary part of the endocrine system attached to the third chakra. Imbalance here has much to do with an unchanneled life force, where there is something deep within holding a person back from really trusting and following the path of intuition. There is often a noticeable stop/go, stop/go lack of fluidity in such a person's life.

Allergies, being in essence an auto-immune disease, represent an attack on ourselves, our self-destructive patterns out of control. In those with persistent allergic reactions, there can be a tendency to be self-judgmental and to deny one's own innate power, especially if controlled by a dominant parent, spouse or lover.

Kidney problems are sometimes a sign of negative thought patterns and will often arise in 'worriers' – people who are putting too much energy into the little things of life rather than focusing on the bigger picture and trusting in the natural order of things. Short-term problems, such as the sudden passing of a stone, are generally related to one specific situation or person to whom one surrenders one's power; longer term degeneration relates to a more deep-rooted belief and fear that one is at the mercy of outside forces.

Indeed, this distinction between long-term and short-term disease applies to all organs. The latter is usually brought on by something occurring within a specific time frame, while the former is a much more deeply rooted, pathological condition.

The Fourth Chakra
As I have already mentioned, this is the center of the heart and the thymus. If this chakra is fully open in a state of

56

balance, health will generally permeate through the whole body. If it is closed, this can allow many serious diseases to take hold within any organism of the body.

Its relationship with the second and third chakras is very important to understand. If the second and third are open, then there will be a natural flow of the life force which comes up through the first chakra. If they are closed in a major way, then this force will be cut off from the fourth energy center and the effectiveness of the heart and the immune system will be impaired.

This is why I spend so much time on the second and third chakras in the practical section of the book for it is the long-term blockages there which close the fourth chakra and allow such serious diseases as cancer and AIDS to take hold.

Cancer has its roots in so many aspects of imbalance, all of which will be addressed later. These include an inability to express and release emotion; an inner sense of isolation and worthlessness; a lack of love and sense of self; a loss of a close relationship, especially in those who tend to live their lives through others.

The one type of cancer specifically associated with this chakra is breast cancer, which is often related to the feeling of not being touched in the deepest parts, whether physical-ly, emotionally or spiritually. This may have something to do with a specific relationship, but may equally arise from a tendency within the individual to be over-protective of herself, to erect a shell around her.

AIDS shares many of the same roots as cancer, with many subtle variations. (See my book, *AIDS & The Healer Within*, for a deeper look at this syndrome.)

The heart, as we all know, is the center of love, and, as the pump which circulates our blood, it also represents the flow of life. Therefore, low blood pressure is associated with not putting energy into the flow which is our life, while high blood pressure is the opposite: suppressing and controlling, which blocks the flow.

The narrowing of one's arteries, (arterio-sclerosis), is a

physical manifestation of the narrowing of one's attitudes. This and other diseases of the heart have a great deal to do with rigidity, resistance to change in life, and, even more so, the inability to accept people as they are. A life based on demanding, conditional 'love' can play havoc within this area, as can any long-term behavior which denies oneself giving or receiving love.

Upper back pain is also associated with an inability to accept love.

The Fifth Chakra
This energy center is associated with the throat, the mouth and all aspects of the respiratory system, as well as metabolism.

It is, of course, the center of expression and is therefore closely linked to the second chakra and our emotions. For this reason, many emotional blockages physically manifest themselves in this area, especially in the lungs. Bronchitis, pneumonia, tuberculosis, lung cancer and many other such diseases all tend to arise because of the suppression and denseness of emotions deep within a person. Asthma has a similar cause, although this is mainly brought about, especially in children, by being stifled and emotionally suffocated.

Addiction to smoking is an extension of this. Picking up another cigarette is a means of filling a void, often caused by a difficulty in relating really deeply with other people and of expressing oneself in an open way. It is not only the nicotine and tar which cause lung cancer; it is mainly the deeper lack of expression which lies behind the habit.

Most complaints of the throat are also to do with the lack of expression, especially associated with close relationships, while problems in the mouth are often linked with a tendency to express oneself in a negative, critical, even self-critical manner.

Stiffness in the neck and shoulder area will often indicate an inflexible approach to one's means of self-expression, where one limits oneself within certain pre-conceived norms rather than allowing the creative juices just to flow. Creativity, in

this case, may be seen as an obligation rather than as a joyful source of self-expression.

Anemia may not seem to have much to do with the throat, but this is linked to metabolism which is associated with the thyroid gland. The inner source of this state can often be related to an unresolved longing for creative expression, due to a fear of going out and expressing oneself.

The Sixth and Seventh Chakras

Finally we come to the seat of the brain, the pituitary and pineal glands, which regulate much of what goes on beneath them, including the central nervous system and endocrine system as a whole.

Any major disease of the nervous system or the muscles which are associated with it, such as multiple sclerosis or Parkinson's disease, tends to be indicative of a general imbalance running down the whole length of the spinal chord and therefore including all the chakras.

However, the fundamental imbalance within these cases, as with any disease associated with the brain, reflects a deep imbalance between the rational and intuitive sides of a person, generally with the rational far outweighing the intuitive.

A stroke, for instance, tends to afflict those who are very rigid within their perception of life, where they must always see a rational reason for doing something. These are the people who resist their intuitive sense for so long that they ultimately lose touch with it.

Continuous headaches, migraine and insomnia are all caused by the rational mind running riot with minimal intuitive sense to counterbalance it. Headaches and migraines will often occur within people who put too much emphasis on the self, especially those who must analyze and submit to rational scrutiny everything which they experience and do. They are often the kind of people who think very deeply about life, but who focus on every single detail rather than allowing themselves to follow their intuitive feelings.

Insomniacs have similar problems in that all the little details of life will not give them rest as they try to sleep.

Obviously, there are many other diseases which I have not mentioned, and, as I wrote at the beginning of this chapter, these are only supposed to be rough guidelines, which may possibly give you a clue as to one of the sources of imbalance within you at any given time.

If you are affected by a certain disease or by a pain in a specific area of your body, it is always important for you to try and recognize what tends to worsen the symptoms – especially if this can be related to what is going on within you in an emotional or psychological sense. If a certain type of inner stress aggravates the condition, it is likely that this will also be connected to the original source of imbalance.

This chapter brings to an end the 'Understanding' section of this book. If parts of what I have written so far appear to be a little hard to grasp intellectually, do not worry about this. The important thing is just to have a feel for the full potential of The Healer Within. The rest, I trust, will unravel as you pass through the various stages of Practicing The Healer Within.

2

Practicing the
Healer Within

The Physical, the Earth and the First Chakra

In our physical form, we are continuously bombarded by a whole host of outside forces throughout our lives – each thing we come face to face with we must confront or react to in one way or another. Sometimes, we try and shy away from some of the choices we have to make, but, in the end, the way in which we react to these major choices shapes the course of our life. There is no escape from this physical reality and the responsibility we have for our own lives. It is a law of the universe that all that we leave unresolved in our lives will at some point return to confront us again, albeit in another form.

Also, as physical beings in human form, we are an integral part of the planet on which we live. As our civilization has supposedly evolved and we have begun to see ourselves as separate from, even masters of, nature and the earth, so we have lost an understanding of the earth that many ancient cultures had – not just in terms of herbs and their benefic effect on the body, but how we can draw healing energy from the earth itself.

Just as all our cells are living entities unto themselves and are also an integral part of our body, so are we humans individuals unto ourselves and also an integral part of the planet earth; just as the earth is an individual planet unto itself and also an integral part of our solar system, and so on and so on.

What this means is that we are a fundamental part of a far greater whole, which has an energy that can be drawn on whenever we please, as long as we open ourselves up to feel it.

The way I explain this feeling is always to compare the inherent difference within me when I am in the country, rather than the city. Having been an urban dweller for the last half of my life, I have become very accustomed to the way my mind behaves when I am in the city. There is a continuous tendency for the mind to flit from one thing to another, as there are always so many possibilities, so many choices, so much going on. In the country, there is a greater sense of tranquillity, often too much so for the hardened city dweller!

But, the difference goes far beyond there being things to do and not to do. There is a fundamental difference in energy and the reason I am dwelling on this point has a lot to do with that dividing line between health and sickness. That difference is what is called *grounding*.

Let us return once more to that wonderful feeling which runs through you when standing on a beautiful deserted beach. There, standing upon the earth, you are taking in the whole scene with all your senses, not just the visual, and, in opening yourself up with that sense of wonder or appreciation, you are subconsciously connecting yourself to the earth. In reality, you are allowing that earth energy to enter into you through that first chakra, and the rush that you feel is indeed the healing energy of the earth.

If you are sceptical about this, just go to a favorite area that you associate with peace and tranquillity, whether it be in the country or a city park. Sit with your feet on the ground, just allow your mind to go blank and feel the energy of the trees and all around you just become part of you. I will lead you through a meditation to do this at the end of the chapter, but the most important thing is just being *aware*, opening yourself up to the pleasure of your senses all combined together.

If you are constantly in an urban environment with concrete underfoot and all around, living fifteen floors up, your contact with the earth is bound to be minimal. What this means is that there is little to counteract all the constant pressures and variety of an urban lifestyle, where the mind is always active and flitting from one thing to another: there is no base, no fundamental grounding point.

This, in itself, leads to a state of imbalance, particularly if you are going through a major period of inner change or if you are physically sick. With all the turbulence going on within your being in an emotional, psychological or spiritual sense, there must be a physical counterbalance. Without this, you are like a pyramid trying to balance on its apex rather than standing on its solid base.

This is why I always advise city dwellers who cannot or do not want to go out into the country to at least try and spend a certain amount of time each week in a park and feel the earth beneath their feet. This is especially beneficial in areas where there are trees.

If you study trees closely, you will see what wonderful transformers of energy they are and how they in a certain way mirror that physical/spiritual duality within ourselves. There they stand, upright and strong, drawing nutrition from the earth and energy from the sun.

If you are not worried about what people think of you, just go up to a tree sometime, put your arms around it as if you are hugging it and rest your head against the trunk, closing your eyes. Whenever I do this, especially if my head is in a whirl from too much activity, I feel as if all unwanted thoughts and worries spiral out of my head, down the tree trunk into the earth, and are replaced by a sense of timelessness and well-being.

Try it sometime. Do not expect any specific feeling. Just let it flow!

Problems associated with the lower limbs are often associated with a lack of grounding and the results of this lack.

65

The most common accidents happen to the joints, ligaments and bones of the leg, in particular ankles and knees. But, of course, accidents are never pure chance; there is always an inner lesson to learn from them.

When I sprained my ankle this last summer, I had just moved up to the country. But, in the month of August, I had arranged to run around doing so many things that I had scheduled very little time to spend in the peace of the country. I sprained my ankle on August 1st and was forced to spend most of the month in the country on crutches!

Problems with the ankles almost always occur in order to tell us that we are going off in too many directions at the same time and are fundamentally ungrounded, needing to focus our energy much more within ourselves rather than towards the outer details of our lives.

Our feet in general are of course our primary contact with the earth. They represent our progress in physical terms and any problems related to them tend to be associated with a reluctance to 'step forward' in our lives.

Problems with our knees, on the other hand, usually mean a certain amount of inflexibility in this stepping forward, in particular if we march blindly on along a single, narrow track, choosing to ignore anything else which may cross our path and lead us to explore other avenues and possibilities.

Another specific area related to the first chakra and grounding is the lower back. When describing the first chakra, I mentioned that it was associated with our instinct for survival and security. If we feel at any time that this security is threatened, in particular in a financial sense, there is a tendency in many people for a pain to develop in the lower back region above the coccyx bone. Fundamentally, the only way for this to be eliminated forever is to learn to trust and believe that you can create your own prosperity. This is, in a sense, a barometer of your current faith in the Healer Within: if you cannot believe in your own ability to create prosperity on the most basic material level, there is still a lot of work to do in order to mobilize the Healer Within.

Many of us see work as a 'necessary evil' and money in particular as the 'root of all evil' – the very antithesis of spirituality. To those of you who do feel this, I say: 'Get over it!'

Our material prosperity is as much a reflection of the harmony and balance within our lives as our emotional and physical well-being. If we are condemning money as the 'root of all evil', we are once again falling into the trap of seeing our spiritual and physical lives as distinct rather than unified energies. If you condemn what money stands for, then that part of your life will never be easy for you. It is much simpler to welcome prosperity into your life and then make the money you earn work for the common good.

The work or job we do is also an important factor in bringing our spiritual and physical lives into harmony and balance. In the ideal world, this work is the true expression of our creativity, but I acknowledge that this is not always the case. As with all the states of being upon which I shall focus in this book, our means of earning money is a reality which we have the power to create when the time is right.

Work also has the very specific function of being a grounding activity in itself. We tend to go through the experiences which cause the most profound changes in us at times when we are not working. These are the periods when we are 'free' and our activities are expansive in nature, whether in terms of learning, developing human relationships or whatever.

Work is a counterbalance to all this activity and plays an important role in allowing this experience to be assimilated into our being – (as long as work is not addictive, in which case it stifles all inner growth). In my own experience, I have always needed periods when I have been busy at work in order to bring me 'down to earth' after periods of intense learning and growth. (Physical exercise fulfils the same function and is important on a regular basis for the same reason.)

We now finally come to the practical side of this book.

I do not say that following the various stages of this

process will instantly bring every aspect of your life into complete harmony. A lot of the imbalance which we all have within us has accumulated over years and years, and we cannot shed this with just a few meditations.

My aim is simply to start or accelerate a process by which you can take your life into your own hands and find that true essence within yourself which will gradually guide you to determine the course of your own existence. I never say the path is easy, but, once begun, it is difficult to turn back.

The meditation below is an introduction for you to focus on the healing power that lies within the earth, as well as the higher vibration of the spiritual energy which flows through us. Although very simple, it is a very powerful meditation which I do every day – it is best done outside, but is equally well done at home. If you do it inside, sit comfortably but upright in a chair with your feet on the floor, close your eyes and just imagine, if you wish, that you are sitting, leaning against a tree trunk, the sun beating down upon you.

MEDITATION NO.1

With your eyes closed, breathe deeply from your diaphragm both in and out, and, as you breathe, focus in on that central part of yourself which is your spinal cord – indeed, see your breath move up and down your spinal cord, slowly up and down.

Once you are comfortable with focusing on your spinal cord, you gradually see it extend downwards out of your body into the earth. You can visualize it in whatever way you want – you may see it purely as your spinal cord coming out of your body, as a bamboo, the root of a tree, a rope with a stone attached to weigh it down, anything as long as it is linking you to the earth.

Slowly, this extension of yourself, this grounding cord goes further and further down into the earth, and, as it does so, you can follow it down, through the various layers of the earth, the soil as we know it with all the living organisms inside, through the various layers of rock, liquid, gas, one on top of each other, deeper and deeper until you feel yourself reaching the hot, liquid core of the earth. And, as you descend, you feel its warm, nurturing quality envelop you.

Leaving this grounding cord rooted in the earth, you return to your body and focus on the soles of your feet, visualizing a small round opening appear in each of them. Then, from the depths of the core of the earth, you see two shafts of energy rising up towards you and entering into your body through these openings in your feet. And the earth energy that you feel is a warm, reddish-brown, heavy energy, almost like the lava that pours out of a volcano.

And this dense, nurturing energy fills your feet, works slowly up your calves, over your knees, expanding through your thighs, over your buttocks and genital area, coming to a rest at your pelvis, so that the whole lower part of your body is filled by this earth energy. Then, as this energy continues to flow, any excess pours back into the earth through your grounding cord from the base of your spine, so that there is a continuous cycle of energy from the earth, up through your feet and down back into the earth.

And then, still continuing to feel this connection to the earth, you turn your attention to the top of your head and see another opening appear at your crown chakra. As you do so, you see coming from some distant part of the universe, whether from the sun, the moon, a star or anywhere far beyond, a brilliant shaft of bright gold light, like a laser beam, shooting into the top of your head through this opening in the crown. And the quality of this energy is much lighter, less dense than the earth energy.

This bouncing gold light completely fills your brain sweeping away in front of it any worries, any dark spots that may have settled there. It fills up the whole of your head, over your eyes, ears, nose, mouth, flowing down over your neck and shoulders, blasting away any tension that may have built up there, and then down your arms to the tips of your fingers.

And the main shaft of this gold, vibrant universal energy shoots downwards into your heart and, as it does so, it blazes forth into the whole upper part of your body through your arteries, cleansing your blood, your lymph system, surrounding your T-cells with a protective ray of healing energy, cleansing your lungs, kidneys and liver, bringing light and balance to your nerves, and, as it flows through all your vital organs, all the dark spots within them, the viruses, whatever should not be there, are swept away with the light and down into the earth.

Then, just sit there a while, feeling those two different currents of energy flow through your body, so that every cell of your body is filled with one or the other: the dense, nurturing energy from the earth as far up as your pelvis, and the bouncing, gold light from above, each radiating health and harmony throughout every part of you.

Finally, in your own time, slowly open your eyes and put your hands to the ground, letting any unwanted energies within you flow out through them.

This healing meditation is to make you aware of those two parts of you: the earthly/physical energy and the universal/spiritual energy. They are both equal parts of you and if you ignore one at the expense of the other, you upset a natural balance within you.

This is what I call the 'maintenance' meditation, not only because I do it very quickly every day, but also because it is necessary to ground yourself in this way before undertaking the other meditations within this book.

If you at first find it difficult, don't worry. Try again and use your own creativity. You may visualize things in a different way. As long as you follow the basic guidelines, just following your own intuition.

One last word about meditating in general. If you find your mind wandering, don't fight it or be hard on yourself. If your mind wanders, be aware of the thought, just let it float away and gradually bring your mind back to focus on that central part of yourself, the spinal cord. If you get angry with yourself or impatient, then your mind will never settle.

The Nurturing Parent

Before I finish this chapter on the first chakra, you will remember that I mentioned that this was the chakra through which we are attached as a child to our nurturing parent and that this connection is a necessary grounding connection for the young infant.

A young child is dependent for its survival on its nurturing parent, usually the mother, and this strong link is a perfectly natural phenomenon. This 'cord' from the first chakra is actually attached to the nurturing parent, in lessening degrees as the child grows older, up till about the seventh year. As the child develops greater independence, this tie loosens and the grounding cord is established in the earth.

Most children then progress through adolescence into adulthood and the relationship between parent and child hopefully becomes a relationship between two adults. Yet, over the years, I have worked on a not inconsiderable number of adults for whom this is not the case: where the relationship towards the parent or parents has remained essentially passive.

When I work on the first chakra of such a person, this comes through very strongly, because there is no link between the first chakra and the earth; instead, I feel the very distinct energy of the parent. Most often, this parent is the mother, but occasionally, especially in the case of women, it can be the father. Deep down within the individual in question is a real need for love and approval from the parent, a need which will often overshadow everything else in the person's life. Usually, such parents are very dominant, sometimes in an aggressive, possessive manner, but just as often in a very quiet, but manipulative way.

Parents will come up quite a lot as this book progresses, but what I want to make clear here is that, if an adult is still tied to his or her nurturing parent's 'apron strings', this means that he or she is not grounded. That connecting point with the earth is instead attached to the parent.

I cannot stress this too strongly: if you are not grounded, you run the risk of any of your bodily systems going out of control, out of balance. Most of us have known someone who has had some kind of nervous breakdown or disorder. That is a typical example of an ungrounded person, someone whose mind whirs away without the strength of the physical side, the earth energy to counteract it.

In some people, a lack of this grounding manifests itself in an external nervous condition, but, more often, it manifests itself less clearly by creating imbalance in the inner workings of the body, such as the endocrine and immune systems.

That is why I am very serious when I say: 'Be aware of the earth', especially if you are looking to heal your life.

Sex

I must say that I am getting rather tired of all the squeaky clean, so-called 'New Age' teachers who give the impression that all will be well in the world if you hug each other and love yourself. They talk about an airy-fairy spirituality which completely fails to take into account that elemental, physical force in our lives which manifests itself in our sexual energy.

Without exception, the most powerful spiritual healers and teachers whom I know of my generation, whether male or female, are also among the most sexual people I know. They are the ones who most strongly acknowledge and tap into the earth energy which flows into our bodies and merges with our spiritual consciousness.

So many religions, and indeed many spiritual healers of the 'old school', view this sexual energy as the very antithesis of spirit and therefore see it as something which should be suppressed or at best swept under the carpet. In seeing the sexual act as merely a means of procreation, they fail to understand or choose to ignore the very nature of human consciousness.

You only have to look at the numerous nature programs on TV to see that the sexual act in the insect and animal kingdom serves as a purely biological function. It is for the most part a very short and peremptory act, quite distinct from all the associations we connect with sex in our own lives. We humans are not purely animal – we are creatures of consciousness and sexuality is a fundamental part of this.

Sex in its highest form is the most wonderful expression of love and intimacy open to us. Do not forget this. We are physical beings and beings of spirit, and sex as an expression of feeling is the fusion of these seemingly distinct aspects of ourselves. I hardly need to remind you of the incomparable sensation which overwhelms your whole being during those moments when it all comes together – especially when that energy rises up to the level of the heart.

From our adolescence well into adulthood, sex is a potent force which drives us onwards to explore the deepest recesses of ourselves and other people. Its natural energy is so powerful that, whenever it is suppressed, the effects of this suppression will rebound in the most disruptive manner, destroying balance within our emotions and physical body.

If it wasn't bad enough having the Catholic church, the hierarchy of which has always used the suppression of our sexual energy as a very effective instrument of power, we now of course have AIDS to contend with, and all the judgment of society which has resulted from this disease.

When one discusses sex and AIDS, that horribly judgmental word 'promiscuity' always seems to crop up. But, what really is promiscuity? In a strict definition, I suppose it means having sex with lots of different partners, but what is it that really lies behind such behavior?

I have already written about how we are 'trapped' within our physical body. In our day to day lives, we learn and grow from our interreaction with our fellow men, and, being physical beings, we all have that strong and perfectly natural desire for physical connection and intimacy. This is a natural extension of our physical form and the life force which runs through us.

This physical connection can be withdrawn from us in many ways and at many different stages of our lives. We may have had parents who never showed us physical affection; we may have been brought up with the feeling that sex is something dirty or not to be talked about; we may

have fallen in love and been rejected by our lover. Any such deprivation may create within us a need for physical intimacy which can become all-consuming if we do not recognize the source of this need.

Whatever the background, so-called promiscuity has always, in my experience, arisen from the search to find that intimacy, to lose oneself in another person. Once we have experienced the real intensity of this feeling, we will often yearn to recapture it; but, the trouble can be that, for many, men in particular, the memory that remains is often of the physical aspect of sex, rather than the depth of feeling which lay behind it – especially after a relationship has broken up, when the feeling has so often turned to anger or sorrow, and all that remains is the physical memory.

What can then arise is a subconscious need to recapture the best moments of what has been lost and that need can certainly become so all-consuming that the initial desire for intimacy is lost and the quest for physical release takes over. If there is an accompanying sense of guilt, the whole process can become a cycle which is difficult to break.

What I want to stress is that there is nothing intrinsically evil or wrong in having sex with many different partners. Obviously, there is nowadays the added necessity of taking certain physical precautions, but sexual relationships, like all our relationships, are an important means of exploring and understanding our own natures. Those who use AIDS as an excuse for giving up sex are actually just giving in to the fear of that unbridled energy and intensity of emotion which sex represents for them.

A major part of what we can learn from sex is recognizing what are the true motivations and emotions which lay behind sex for us, including the type of energy it is that we put into a sexual relationship or encounter.

Just think a little about what these are for yourself. Then, be perfectly honest with yourself and mark below those which apply to you in one way or another. You can add others if you wish.

Sex is:

☐An expression of love for one particular person.
☐An expression of love, intimacy and warmth with any person.
☐A way of getting close to someone more quickly.
☐A means of finding a lover.
☐A way of overcoming loneliness, of filling a void, a need within yourself.
☐An adventure: the thrill of a new encounter.
☐A means of escape from the day to day reality of your life.
☐A way of releasing pent up energy and tension.
☐A way of proving your own self-worth, your own attractiveness.
☐A means of exerting power or control over someone or having someone do the same over you.
☐Getting your rocks off – a purely physical sensation.

Also, I ask you to be aware of what sex has meant to you in the past, what it means to you now and what you want it to mean to you. Do you now view sex as good or bad, healthy or unclean, a natural impulse or something that should be suppressed? All this is important for you to understand.

Having written a book on AIDS, I have obviously worked with many people with AIDS, and, of course, the question of sex will usually come up at some point.

The one thing I stress again and again is that AIDS is not here to teach us that sex, in particular gay sex, is bad. In fact, in my experience, AIDS has made many of us look more deeply at what sex does really mean to us and we have therefore learned to value and appreciate it more.

One of the saddest aspects of this epidemic is the self-judgment and feeling of guilt which is so prevalent within many people with AIDS – they have taken upon themselves the judgment of society, instead of valuing and nurturing their own sexual natures. Guilt is something which I shall discuss shortly, but its essence is surrendering your own power to the opinions of others. It is probably the most destructive emotion there is and can cause havoc within the human body and psyche.

With regard to any sexual situation, I ask you to let go of guilt instantly. If you have sex with someone, even a one night stand, and the communication and feelings were there, and it *felt* right, then there is no reason for self-judgment. If, on the other hand, you find yourself in a sexual situation which gives you no pleasure or even drains your energy, then understand what causes this sensation and learn from it, so that you do not need to go through the same again, and, for that matter, put your partner through the same.

Because of the immense power of this physical energy which is there deep within all of us, it can be an incredibly positive, healing force within our whole being. *Sex as an expression of love and intimacy is one of the strongest healing energies we can bring into our bodies*, as it is the sharing of life force between two people: a union more powerful than any external medicine that a doctor can prescribe for us.

However, the power of this physical energy is a double-edged sword in that its energy will equally highlight an imbalance within an individual. If our sexual behavior is hiding some fear or emotion suppressed deep within us, the resulting imbalance will be more prone to take root within our bodies.

The following is a scenario of the life of someone just before he came down with AIDS. I shall call him Peter, but he could be many people – not just people with AIDS but anyone for whom sex is an important issue.

Peter has had one major relationship in his life and a few minor ones, but, at this moment, he is alone. Deep down, he still yearns for the warmth, comfort and intimacy that relationships bring. He goes out to a bar – it does not matter if this is a gay bar or a straight single's bar – and he looks for someone to take home with him. And then, it seems that he is doing this rather a lot. He does not always meet somebody, and, even if he does, it does not necessarily satisfy him. In fact, the more he does it, the greater the feeling of emptiness inside him. Even so, he continues to go out, because the fear of loneliness is even stronger within him.

In short, it becomes a habit. After a while, he loses any expectation of lasting tenderness from any of these encounters. If he stays in at night, he has his collection of dirty movies, so that he can fantasize about his ideal, physical sexual experience. When he goes out, he goes looking for a certain type, and when he brings this type home, he sees his partner as a sexual outlet with whom he can play out his fantasies. Deep down, he regrets not being able to become more intimate, but he has got so used to projecting a certain image of himself that he is afraid of exposing any vulnerability.

And then, wham, he gets sick.

Of course, there is a lot going on within Peter and most of it has the effect of causing imbalance in his life and within his body. Cumulatively, the effect is devastating.

Let me explain bit by bit.

1. First of all, there is that feeling of emptiness. We have all felt emptiness to a certain extent at some point in our lives and don't fool yourself: you can be doing something every moment of your waking life and still feel that emptiness. The emptiness that Peter is feeling principally derives from the fact that he is looking for someone to fill that void. In the end, it is sex, rather than a personal relationship that fills the void and then only for short spaces of time.

AIDS, cancer, any major disease feeds on that harrowing feeling of emptiness, of isolation. For those of you who have undergone periods where you have felt that there is nothing really within your life which is lasting and gives you joy, you know the havoc it wreaks on your moods and your body.

Where there is emptiness and indifference in your life, this means that you have lost a sense of your true essence, that consciousness which is your own. And where there is no consciousness, the 'consciousness' of any disease can enter.

2. Where sex becomes a habit for whatever reason and

the sexual act is not a shared *feeling* with your partner, then you open yourself up to a whole host of energies. When you reach the point of orgasm and that incredible physical feeling engulfs the whole of your body and mind, your second chakra opens so wide that it engulfs the rest of your body. The fusion between two people having sex is not purely physical: what actually occurs is that energies on a non-physical plane are exchanged between the two partners through the second chakra.

If the sexual act is part of something deeper, where you are giving and receiving warmth and affection to each other, that exchange of energies is also on a heart level and can only be positive.

However, in Peter's case, the warmth has gone out of the sex; he has lost a sense of the individual person with whom he is having sex and it is just as likely that his partner too will be seeing him in much the same way: as an image, as a means of fulfilling a physical desire.

What happens in such circumstances is that Peter is opening himself up to any negative energies that may be coming from his partner, just as he is giving any within himself to his partner. If this happens regularly, then the power of these outside forces builds up inside him, once more creating imbalance within him.

That is why I say: 'Be aware of what sex means to you'. Like attracts like and, if you are using sex for any other reason than a sense of intimacy and warmth, it is more than likely that your partner will be doing the same, feeding any imbalance which is already inside you.

3. Peter, in trying to attract a certain type, is essentially playing a game and putting a mask over his true self.But, this is no game, as the mask can take over and he loses touch with what is his true essence, the human loving part of himself. Then, fear sets in and he is basically afraid to show any vulnerability or express any emotion.

Then, those true feelings that we all have within us are trapped deep down and are left to smoulder, unacknowledged, unexpressed.

All of these traits of behavior amount to a suppression of that true spirit of love and warmth which is not only fundamental to our being but also to our well-being. Think back to the link that I made between the thymus and the heart center and you will understand that the suppression of that loving part of you means also the suppression of much more, including our immune system.

The way we relate to others is a reflection of the way we relate to ourselves and, in the long run, to our bodies.

The essence of sex and sexuality is the expression of that warm, loving part of ourselves which is in itself our essence. The following short meditation is to make us feel the difference between the purely physical and the deeper aspects of our sexuality.

MEDITATION NO.2

Just close your eyes, and, as before, focus on that central part of yourself. Then, focus on that particular area of your second chakra just below your navel and feel that whirlpool of energy that goes within your body. As you do so, see yourself come out of your body and shrink down in size so that you can walk in through that hollow space that is your second chakra.

When you walk into that space, you find yourself in a dark room. It is dark apart from a bright light in the center of the room and, as you walk up to the light, you see an image of yourself there. And as you see yourself, you bring anyone else into the light and turn the scene into what is your ultimate physical, sexual fantasy. Forget about any emotional connection; let your purely physical imagination run riot and feel within you the sex getting hotter and hotter, the light getting brighter and brighter, so that you can see every detail as if in a mirror, until the energy becomes so intense that

80

it explodes and, all of a sudden, it is over and the light is gone and the darkness returns.

And, as you are in the middle of this dark room, alone, you see in a far corner a faint glow that had been overshadowed by the bright light. You gently walk over to it and, as you get closer, you see once more an image of yourself with someone, but, this time, it is a softer image and you are wrapped in the arms of your partner. The person whom you bring into this gentle glow is the one with whom you have had the most loving, warm and intimate sex and you see yourselves exploring and opening up to each other with tenderness and feeling, kissing, slowly making love, and, as you do so, this sense of warmth, of equally giving and receiving spreads to the area around your heart and you feel your heart center opening up and expanding and expanding, sending rays of warmth and peace throughout the whole of your body until the physical image and the feeling of openness and intimacy become one within you.

Then, for as long as you want, you hold onto that image and sensation, letting it flow through the whole of your body, knowing that you can attract and create this for yourself, and, whenever you feel yourself being obsessed by the physical image of sex, you can return to this other warmer image, the true expression of yourself.

And, finally, you turn around and leave this room, return to your body and open your eyes.

Sex is such an important part of our make-up that it should *never* be ignored. Because our sexual energy is so difficult to control, it offers the greatest challenge in the path towards integrating the physical and spiritual parts of ourselves.

If you look at the underlying feelings behind sex within a human being, you will see that this desire for intimate connection is, in its highest degree, a reflection of our natural desire to be at one with God or the Universe.

Sex is, for many of us, a way of confronting what lies most deeply hidden within us, and sexual expression can be a very important part of raising our energy and vibration up towards our higher self. There are many ways in which sex can help us to start off on that path and, before I move on to the chapter on sexuality, I would like to recommend Mantak Chia's two books which illuminate this path with very specific exercises: *Taoist Secrets of Love: Cultivating Male Sexual Energy & Cultivating Female Sexual Energy* (Aurora Press, New York).

Sexuality: the Male and Female Within All of Us

It is generally accepted that men and women relate to sex in a different way, and this is reflected in the positions of the sex glands. The tests hang outside the framework of the body, representing an energy which is essentially outward going and active; the ovaries lay deep within the body, representing an energy which is essentially receptive and passive.

This does not mean that all men are active and all women passive. It just means that there are two distinct aspects of sexuality: the male and the female, or, as Jung described them, the animus and the anima.

The animus within us is that part of us which is active, assertive and essentially rational; the anima is the passive, nurturing and essentially intuitive side of us. To say that one is the domain of man and the other the domain of woman is absurd, yet many of us have been brought up not to acknowledge the part of us which is not associated with our sex. This is of course changing, as women are allowed to have their own aspirations and goals and men are slowly permitting themselves to show the warm, emotional side of their nature. But, despite these changes, for many people, these old stereotypes still hold true.

The extreme animus character is the macho type who is dominant, aggressive, intolerant and unable or unwilling to express feeling; the extreme anima character is moody, indecisive, 'bitchy' and manipulative. Within both of them, the problem is exactly the same: the extreme animus completely denies and suppresses the anima part of him and *vice versa*. As with any suppression, the imbalance this causes sooner or later makes its way to the physical plane and affects the health of the body.

Despite the scorn it has attracted from many levels of society, homosexuality has given people a much more practical understanding of the fusion of the male and the female, the animus and the anima within one person. In a strange kind of way, rejection by society has given homosexuals a distinct advantage in life in that they do not feel pressured to conform to the role models of this society. A man can show his feminine qualities and a woman can display her masculine traits without the concern over what others think.

It is no coincidence that there is a long shamanic and healing tradition within homosexuals which goes back to the most ancient civilizations. The reason for this is that a healer becomes more powerful as all the different aspects of duality within him or her become unified – and one of the most vital aspects of unity is the bringing together as one the male and female within each of us.

For our own inner harmony and growth, it is extremely important to recognize whether we lean more towards the animus or anima, and, in doing so, try to balance the one with the other. This summer, I spent a lot of time with a woman friend of mine and gradually began to see how each of us still in certain ways fit into the male and female types of behavior.

Throughout my life, there has always been an excess of animus in me, although this has finally diminished. As an intelligent child, I grew up putting a lot of emphasis on my rational mind which tended to judge people and over-form my existence. Due to my background, I always had problems in expressing my emotions, being conditioned to believe that this was not a 'masculine' way to behave. Therefore, I would always have a tendency to suppress my feelings rather than openly and immediately react to a given situation, which would in turn build up as resentment and have deeper effects within my psyche.

There was also that part of me which wanted to control every aspect of my existence, and when something turned out successfully, there would often be an excess of pride in me – not so much pride in something well done, but that competitive pride of having done better than someone else and having proven myself in other people's eyes.

All of these types of behavior represent an excess of animus, the archetype of which is the 'macho' man, who huffs and bluffs his way through life, never showing to anyone how he feels, unless he occasionally feels compelled to act in an aggressive, 'masculine' way to a situation or person which invades his territorial space. The predatory, sexual nature of a man is also an illustration of this extreme.

What is particularly sad about this extreme is that every being has feelings, and the inability to express them means cutting yourself off from your true loving nature. This is why men are so much more prone to heart disease than women, because they deny themselves the warmth, love and compassion which are necessary for the heart to expand and flow.

But, we must also remember that such behavior is not solely the domain of men. I have encountered a considerable number of women who mirror these traits, in particular those who try to succeed in traditionally male dominated territories. Indeed, once obsessed with competing in a male-dominated world, they will often strive to outdo men in their maleness. Margaret Thatcher is a typical case in point.

The other side of the coin is the extreme of anima, of the female nature. In a physical sense, the animus represents form, while the anima represents substance. I have found in my experience that people who are obese or who are excessively overweight are those who deny the animus, male part of them, for there is no form to contain the physical substance of their body. This can apply to a man as much as to a woman.

The extremes of anima come in as many shapes and forms as their male counterpart. Passivity is one, whereby there is an inclination to allow oneself to be blown around by the winds of change and to be dominated by other, usually extreme animus, individuals. This is often accompanied by a complaining nature, so that a person whines about his or her lot rather than doing something about it.

This is particularly dangerous in a person who gets sick or is in a state of emotional turmoil, as it is the very antithesis of the energy behind the Healer Within. It is the mentality that: 'I knew that, if someone was going to get sick, it would be me. That's just the way my life is.' Such people will always be finding fault in and 'bitching' about other people, rather than looking deeply into themselves. In seeing everything beyond their control, they lose any sense of responsibility for their lives and do nothing to deal with the source of a problem.

Whereas an excess of animus will often mean an over judgmental nature towards the outer aspects of life, an excess of anima can cause a lack of judgment for oneself. The friend I mentioned above is one of the most wonderfully non-judgmental people I know towards other people, yet her crisis of this summer was all connected with her inability to judge what was right for herself and to follow a path of her own choosing. This manifests itself in that continuous prevarication and indecisiveness of: 'Shall I do this or shall I do that or maybe it'll be easier if I do nothing at all.'

This can be compounded by that state of suspension where one does not actively choose who to have as close friends. Extreme anima people will often allow anyone to come into their space without considering whether this is a person he or she wants to be close to. This again reflects an inability to judge for oneself and to trust one's intuition rather than always feeling *obliged* to be all things to all people.

Which brings me on to the last aspect of the anima on which I wish to focus. The mentality which makes one always feel obliged to give in to others can often, in a bizarre way, lead to another extreme: possessiveness. How often I have seen mothers, in particular in Latin or Jewish families, who will on the surface always be at the beck and call of their men folk, yet who in reality are the dominant force in the family. There is a manipulative quality to this behavior, whereby they appear to be passive, but manage to quietly direct things in such a manner that they always get their way in the major decisions! I have always found this quite an art to watch!

Yet, the effect of this manipulation can be quite devastating, where the mother appears to give the family freedom to do what they want, but instills an incredible feeling of guilt within them when they stray from the prescribed path. I have seen this have a drastic, long-term effect on many children and the irony of it all is that such manipulative, 'anima' mothers, nearly always produce the most macho, aggressive, 'animus' sons. The process turns full circle!

So, as you can see, the extremes of animus and anima can have a far-reaching effect on countless aspects of our lives and each of these extremes represents another source of imbalance within us, which necessarily holds us back from activating the Healer Within. If you see any of these extremes within yourself to any extent, just be aware of them and slowly try to bring them into balance. But, do not be hard on yourself, as that will only make it worse!

Just for a moment think of yourself as a totally balanced being in this respect and feel the completeness within you. Think first of all of that receptive, loving part of you which values the warmth of human contact, the caring shown by real friends; then consider that active part of you, your own creativity and your ability to go out and create your own reality, express yourself in your own individual way. Then, just close your eyes and see yourself in harmony with the outside world, giving and receiving *equally*. There is no reason to deny any part of ourselves, and even less reason not to show to the world the way we truly are.

Emotions and Pain

I have written about some of the emotions that come into play with sex and sexuality, yet, of course, emotions are aroused by many different sources. What I intend to show in this chapter is how our emotions tend to relate back to very distinct individuals and events in our lives and how they can act as a dead weight around us, if we don't let them go. We can carry anger, guilt, jealousy, sorrow, fear and a whole host of other emotions around with us for a lifetime, but, if we do so, like an uncleaned wound, they can fester inside us and infect the whole of our body.

As mentioned earlier, all of us at some point in our lives have some period of intense suffering and pain or go through an experience which makes an immense impact upon us. These are generally the times of our lives when we become introspected and therefore learn most about ourselves. They also often give us the extra strength to deal with any other hardship that may come along.

Our emotions are nearly always wrapped up with the memory of such events and, more specifically, with particular people who have had influence over us. One of the consequences of our rational mind is that we have a tendency to dart from the past to the future and back to the past rather than remaining in the stillness of the present moment. Retaining a memory of a bad experience is not totally a bad thing, as we have probably learnt from the experience. What does us harm, however, is holding on to the *emotional charge* of the experience.

I am often asked what I mean about emotional charge, so let me explain. Let us assume that I have been in a supposedly monogamous relationship for three years and my lover tells me that he or she has fallen in love with someone else and has indeed been having sex with that person for three months. Now, I had realized that our relationship had been coming to an end for a while, but it had just seemed too harsh a change to suddenly break it off and be alone again. So, when my lover tells me this, a whole host of emotions overwhelm me: anger at the dishonesty and betrayal; jealousy and hurt ego that my lover had gone off with someone else; sorrow and pain and a certain amount of fear and self-pity that I was now left alone.

Of course, deep down, we all know that 'time heals' and we ultimately recognize that a certain relationship was a transition period and was not meant to last, but many of us allow the emotional charge of the experience of loss to obliterate this knowledge. Instead of understanding that such an experience was part of learning and growing, we sometimes hold on to the emotions which were left in its wake, and, as they lie simmering in the recesses of our mind, they become embittered.

We may often think that we have let go of this 'emotional charge', but then we behave in a certain way which demonstrates that we have not. Sometimes, this may manifest itself in a reluctance to commit to a relationship through the fear of being hurt again, or, on the other end of the spectrum, we may enter into a period of promiscuity in search of the warmth of human touch which we have lost. We may find ourselves being angered by certain behavior in others, because it reminds us of someone who has caused us pain. The list goes on forever.

This is what I mean by holding on to the emotional charge of an experience. Just one major event or relationship in the past which has caused great pain or suffering can, if not released, start off a pattern within us which robs us of our own inner strength. By holding on to such an event, or more often the person associated with it, we are quite simply giving it power over us. In particular, if the feelings involved remain unacknowledged and unexpressed, the pressure within grows and grows like the pressure that builds up gradually between two geological plates before an earthquake. And that earthquake could be anything in your life. It could be a life threatening disease.

To illustrate this, let me give an example of a person who came to see me once. The first thing I immediately became aware of within him was an immense anger that had obviously built up over many years. I told him what I felt and he vehemently denied that he felt any anger towards anyone in his life.

So, I went on to other things that were relevant to him and gradually edged my comments around to his parents. Suddenly, the floodgates of resentment opened. Out poured a whole history of conflict and some particularly devious and persistent behavior by his parents that was designed to keep him under their power.

'So, you don't feel any anger then?' I asked him. 'I've never really thought of me being angry. I resent them, I suppose,' came the reply.

It's funny how we can play games with ourselves, even with words, but all it means is that we so often bury things deep within us. There is of course nothing new in this, as any psychologist will tell you, but the way in which we consciously or subconsciously deny fundamental parts of our being and, in doing so, give them power over us, not only affects our behavior but also the strength within us that enables us to maintain health within our bodies: the Healer Within.

In this particular case, the unresolved resentment towards his parents filtered through into every aspect of his life: nothing or nobody was ever quite right. If something bad happened to him, it was just bad luck, it wasn't fair; it certainly was not anything of his own doing. And, deep down, he felt that if anyone was going to get sick, it was

bound to be him.

Quite simply, he had surrendered his power to the extent that, even when he recognized this, he went from one treatment and nutritionist to another, doing everything but look for the strength within himself.

Now, this may seem to be a very harsh and judgmental portrait but if we all look deep within ourselves, most of us will recognise how, to some degree, we have or still do allow a certain experience or person in our lives to remain as a blockage within our inner selves. Anger is often the easiest emotion to recognize because of its explosive energy and is therefore the easiest to deal with, but there are many other less obvious and often more insidious ways in which we react to so-called negative experiences and influences in our lives.

One of the most common of these is quite simply to suppress any emotional reaction and deny that someone or some situation has had any effect on you whatsoever. I must confess that I used to be very much like this, and this came very much to the fore when I sprained my ankle this summer.

I was given a reading on my sprained ankle by a healer friend of mind and she told me that, as well as giving me the obvious message that I was rushing around too much, the sprain was pointing me towards a more important, long-term imbalance. She said that all the emotional stuff that I had not dealt with throughout my life was locked up in my joints and this had to be released if I was to achieve the sense of harmony and flow I was seeking.

So, I was given the following instructions. I was to start with my sprained ankle, and, revolving it slowly, I was to empty my mind and breathe gently and deeply with my attention focused on that joint, allowing anything to come to the surface of my thoughts.

I did this for a while and nothing spectacular happened, but, gradually, especially after I had stopped revolving the ankle and just sat there, gently breathing, certain poignant memories from the past started to come to the surface. My instructions were to do this once or twice a day for about three days or as long as it felt necessary and then to move on to the next joint and do the same. So, I started with my ankles and toes, each side in turn, moving up to my knees, pelvis, fingers, wrists, elbows etc. and finally up to my shoulders and neck.

As I went through this process, I found that different joints concealed different types of emotional experiences, some more intense than others. All in all, though, I was amazed how many experiences and particular periods of my life, especially from my childhood, came up out of the blue – mostly those times in my life that I had long forgotten about or, more to the point, shoved away into the deepest recesses of my being.

I would recommend this to anyone of you who feels that there is much unresolved business lying deep within you, but before you do so, understand that you are making a commitment to understanding and releasing a lot of stuff that you had subconsciously chosen to keep hidden. During that period that I was undertaking this task, I had more intense dreams and nightmares than during any period of my life that I can remember. Yet, with each stage, I would slowly begin to feel lighter and freer. Also, the understanding of the inner pain that I had suppressed made me understand what lay behind certain aspects of my present behavior which I wanted to release.

If you have or know anyone who has severe or even slight arthritis, rheumatism, or degenerative bone disease, this aching pain will exist on the physical level because of pain on the emotional and psychological level which has been allowed to lie festering within these joints for years. Evidently, at this advanced stage, the pain is more ingrained and therefore more difficult to release; in these circumstances, the process must be done much more slowly and gradually, focusing on one joint at a time over a longer period of time. (Even if there is no physical pain, you should not rush from one joint to the other, as this will not give the time or space for complete assimilation and release to take place, and may cause excess stress to your system.)

And remember, it is not just the revolving of the joint that is important; it is by directing one's whole consciousness into the joint that one creates the energy to effect the release.

Extreme physical pain, such as I felt with my kidney stone, is probably the one thing we fear most of all when we think of illness.

Even pain does not come to us by chance. Severe pain comes to us as a 'last resort' in that it blocks everything else out of our physical, emotional and mental senses, creating a vacuum which allows releasing to take place on subtler planes. Pain equals resistance. If we are in pain, this means that we are holding on to something, usually of an emotional nature, which is holding us back from the natural flow which guides us forwards in our lives.

Short-term, sharp pains are often a means of creating a release on a subconscious plane, because the person in question is unable or unwilling to do this on a conscious level. However, if you or someone you know is in long-term pain, there is often much work to do on both planes.

In such cases, physical pain is a reflection of pain which is felt on a much deeper level. It may well be that the source of this pain has been buried deep in your subconscious, and, as with the exercize I have just recommended with your joints, focusing your consciousness on the particular area of physical pain can lead to an understanding and release of its source.

The deeper the emotional pain is buried, the longer the process will take to be effective. Even if nothing immediately comes to the surface, the very act of awareness will begin to create changes which will probably manifest first of all in your dreams. If you keep a pad beside your bed and record your dreams, this will accelerate the process by bridging the gap between the subconscious and the conscious.

If you are close to someone who is terminally ill, it is so important for you to help that person in the understanding that any physical pain will fade if only they will release much of the inner pain which lies deep inside. By trusting in the power of your own words, especially those of love and forgiveness, you will create an energy around a dying person which will ease the process of letting go and allow the transition to the other side to take place in peace.

Forgiveness

Quite simply, forgiveness is the most powerful weapon you have in your inner armory, as it is forgiveness which breaks the hold which any negative emotional attachment from the past has upon you. Yet, for many people, forgiving is the most difficult thing to do, and I am talking just as much about forgiving oneself as forgiving others.

There are many reasons for this. Sometimes, it is pride or, an extension of this, the 'martyr complex', whereby we must show everybody how much we have been hurt. Indeed, there is a very strong contradiction within many of us that makes us hold on to a negative emotional state because it has become so much part of us that it is almost a comfort, a part of our personality that gives us security because it is familiar.

But, what really is forgiveness and what does it have to do with our health?

In simplest terms, and in its most important function as a restorer of balance, it is the release of any negative charge stored in the past; indeed, it is the release of any hold the past has upon us.

I have had many discussions with people, especially students and graduates of psychology, about the relevance of the past. For many psychologists, the past, in particular any negative patterns associated with it, is something first of all to be identified, then submitted to rational scrutiny, understood and to be 'made friends with'.

For me, the past is an encumbrance, excess baggage to be let go of. We are, each and every one of us, an accumulation of the experiences of the past – each major event in our lives makes its mark upon us and shapes us into the beings we are in the present, yet the past remains the past.

People who remain fixated in the past, whether on a negative experience or through a vague nostalgia for 'better times', must necessarily take energy and vitality away from the present life, and, when we are talking about dis-ease, we are talking about the present moment.

This is where forgiveness comes in. The more ingrained a feeling of anger towards someone may be within you, the more a sign of your own strength it is to forgive that person and let go of the emotional charge associated with him or her. By not forgiving and by holding on to the resentment, you are giving that person power over you – the last thing you really want to do.

Now, of course, if you have made a habit over the years of harboring emotions deep within you without expressing, releasing or even recognizing them, it may well seem easier said than done to let go of them just like that. I shall be going much deeper into this problem in the later chapters on power and control, but, for now, I am offering a very simple meditation through which you can visualize and effect the breaking of the bonds between you and another person.

Remember. It is the cycle of life: as you forgive, so will you be forgiven.

MEDITATION NO.3

Once more, close your eyes and focus in on that central part of yourself and breathe gently until you are at peace within yourself.

Then, focus on that area of your second chakra,

just two fingers below your navel and imagine a cord attached to you at that point and this cord stretches off into the distance.

You can then see yourself take hold of this cord and pull it in, and, as you do so, you see, attached to the other end, a person who has hurt you in the past and towards whom you still feel some attachment, whether one of regret, resentment or whatever. It can be a member of your family, an ex-lover, the one individual you associate strongest with inner pain and resentment.

As you see this person standing in front of you, you ask him or her: 'Why is it that you are still attached to me? What is the contract between us?'

You then wait for the answer to come to you. It may come from the image of this person in front of you or it may come from your own inner voice, telling you what the experience between you two taught you or what it was within this person which made he or she behave in this way or what it was in your own behavior that brought out a negative response in the other person. Just take your time in this place of quietness and allow this person and the attachment between you to become clear, unencumbered by any emotional response within you.

Then, see yourself taking this figure in front of you by the hands and saying out loud: 'You no longer have any hold or power over me. I forgive you for all that you have done to me in the past, as this is no longer part of me, and I ask you to forgive me for anything I may have done to hurt you. I release you to your highest good, just as I ask you to release me to mine.

Then, you quite simply tug at the cord that is attached to your second chakra and it comes away easily in your hand. You let go of it and it drifts away, together with the person at the end of it, into the distance out of sight. And you fill the gap left by the pulled out cord with a ray of bright gold light, in the knowledge that this cord can never attach itself there again, drawing vital energy away from you.

Now, it is of course possible that you cannot find someone at the end of this cord and, if not, I suggest that you search deeply, as we all have some resentment towards someone and the least recognized can often be the most powerful. If you still cannot find anyone, good for you. If you do and you find that you cannot let go, just feel how much power you are allowing this person to have over you. Then, try again!

Sorrow, Grief and Bereavement

There are many ways in which people hold on to the emotional charge of a past experience and among the most intense are those people who carry around with them a deep sense of sadness, sorrow and pain, which lies like a darkness in the recesses of their soul.

This is the very antithesis of anger with its bubbling fury and resentment. Anger is associated with the color red, the fire boiling within, while the color of deeply felt sorrow, which has often been carried around like a dead weight for many years, is black, lifeless, almost completely drained of energy, yet no less powerful a disruptive force within the body than the fieriness of anger.

Sadly too, there lies within these heavy souls a strange sense of resignation about disease in general, such that I have heard the following statement: 'I always felt that, if anyone was going to get sick in my circle, it would be me.'

Such is the power of thought and of the depth of suffering that some people hold on to.

Most often, such inner pain is associated with a loss which has overshadowed every other event in a person's life. This can either be the early death of a parent or someone very close or the withdrawal of love by someone upon whom the person depended. In the latter case, this may be the end of a relationship, which in another person may have aroused anger and resentment, but, in this case, the person carries the deep felt pain stoically within.

The energy associated with this is the most extreme example of how holding on to the past can drain and suffocate the healing power within, for the will to live, the sense of joy in life has been eaten away by the feeling, often deep down and unexpressed, that it is their destiny to suffer, to experience sorrow and pain. It is a complete denial of any power within the self, a final surrender to the notion that the individual is at the mercy of cruel destiny.

In someone who is sick already, it is a pattern that needs to be immediately arrested, for the natural progression is for that hidden resignation towards sickness to be closely followed by a resignation towards death.

This 'darkness of the soul' hits me right between the eyes as soon as I encounter it in someone, but it is not always obvious to everybody because of the stoicism that often hides it. Indeed, the extent of it is rarely even understood by the person involved.

Often, this state is betrayed by continuous self-deprecating remarks, for there lies hidden beneath it a sense of not being good enough. When children lose a parent either through death or divorce, it is not uncommon for them to believe that this has happened because they somehow deserved it. However illogical this may seem to an adult, this feeling can be very real and can be subconsciously carried around into adulthood if it is not confronted and released at an early stage.

The same can apply to someone who has been equally affected by the end of an important relationship. If one has invested a lot of emotional energy into a relationship with someone and that person suddenly goes off with somebody else, it is very easy for one to assume the judgment that one is not good enough. Just as in the case of the deserted child, this is a feeling that can be carried around within for years. If this happens, the person in question will always find it difficult to enter into a relationship with someone, as there will always be, in the back of the mind, that nagging feeling of not being good enough and the fear of being deserted again.

Of course, the most intense example of sorrow and grief is generally bereavement, the loss of a loved one. We all have to go through it at some point in our lives, but, more often than not, we are emotionally unprepared for it.

In addition to the sense of loss, there can be so many different emotions involved. If the death is sudden and unexpected, there is all-consuming shock, often accompanied by a sense of injustice. If death comes after the long-lasting stress of looking after a loved one, there is that feeling of emptiness after having expended so much energy and even a vague sense of guilt for not having been able to do enough.

The most important aspect of the grief of bereavement is the expression and sharing of this grief, whether through tears and words with family and friends or even in silent communion with that spiritual part of oneself in a quiet place. Without this expression, the pain cannot be released and will always come back to haunt you at another time.

Even before one is confronted with the loss of a loved one, it is important to come to terms within oneself with the concept of death. Our grief comes from the physical separation and the memories of happy times which we know will not be repeated in this lifetime, but, in dealing with our own mortality as we did in an earlier chapter, we can understand that this separation is only on a physical plane.

Although we must all feel the grief at the loss of a physical presence, our reaction to the death of a loved one, once the intensity of this grief has passed, is a measure of our faith in the unifying force of life around us.

The link between bereavement and cancer is now well established and there are of course a multitude of cases where one partner quickly follows the other into death. This is always a matter of choice, whether conscious or subconscious, and a perfectly valid choice this is, if that choice has willingly involved investing the bulk of one's energy into another person's life.

However, for many people, life goes on. Because there is that physical separation in death, this does not mean that there is a total separation, however difficult it may be for us to really accept the concept of communicating with someone 'on the other side'.

The truth is that such communication cannot fully occur if there is still a sadness, a holding on to the physical memory of someone who has died. The person who has passed on has left behind the physical body and is therefore no longer limited within the physical impression and memories that we hold on to on this side.

When someone close to us dies, the best we can do for them is to offer prayers of release and love to speed him or her through the process of making that journey from the physical into the spiritual realm. In doing this, we not only ease the transition for our loved one, but also open up a channel for us to receive communication back from the other side when the time is right. Shortly after the person's death, we may, if we are open to it, feel their presence in a certain vaguely physical sense, but, thereafter, communication will generally exist on a subconscious plane, helping to guide us in a certain direction.

We are never truly separated from our loved ones, and, if we mourn their loss as if they are gone from us forever, then we are actually creating a false sense of separation. If we open our hearts to their eternal presence, then their spirit will remain with us always.

I shall not dwell on any more examples of our tendency to cling onto sorrow and pain, but shall move on to a particularly powerful meditation in which you can feel within yourself the difference between sorrow and joy, leaving you in no doubt which is your divine right.

MEDITATION NO.4

As before, close your eyes and focus on that central part of yourself and then move down to the area of your second chakra.

This time, you imagine yourself coming out of your body, shrinking down in size and facing your second chakra as if it is a long corridor stretching out in front of you. You walk along the corridor until you come to a door and over this door is written the word: SORROW.

You open the door and enter into the room. As you walk towards the center of the room, you see a young child there by himself, crying, and you realize that this young child is yourself.

As you see this image of you as a child in front of you, you recall the first time in your life that you remember feeling deep sorrow and pain. It may be the separation from someone who was close to you or it may be that someone you loved deserted you when you needed them. Whoever or whatever it may be, bring this person in front of you and ask them why they had to leave you then. Even if you do not receive an answer, take them by the hands or hug them if you like, releasing the sorrow and pain with the words: 'I forgive you for leaving me and understand that the sorrow I felt is now in the past and no longer has any hold on me. I bless you and release you, just as I ask you to do the same for me.'

Once you have done this for the first time, see this image of you as a child gradually grow up and as it passes through the various stages of your life, through adolescence, the first 'broken heart', all the painful memories of the past, confront them and let go of the emotional charge that surrounds them. Do not also forget to bring into this room and release those who have told you that sorrow must for whatever reason be part of your life and if one of those people is yourself, then release this image of yourself too.

Continue this until finally the figure opposite you is you as you are now.

There is no need to hurry this. Do not leave any stone unturned. Be aware of the strength of emotion surrounding each sorrowful experience and allow this to dissolve into thin air, releasing you from its hold.

Then, once you are satisfied that you have brought into this room everybody whom you associate with sorrow, grief and pain, take a deep breath and with a loud, expressive sigh, see each and every one of them being blown out of the room and far away into the universe by the force of this sigh. And, if you feel reluctant to let them go, understand that it is only the sorrow associated with their memory that you are releasing, not the happy moments you spent together.

So, finally, you are in this room of sorrow by yourself once more, and as you stand in the center of this room, you reclaim your power and say out loud: 'I now leave sorrow and pain behind and understand that these need never enter into my life again. I am at peace within myself and am worthy of a life filled with happiness and joy.'

And then, you leave this room, closing the door behind you.

You then walk a little further down the corridor and come to a door behind which you feel a sparkling energy of lightness and fun. You see above the door the words: JOY, LAUGHTER, SATISFACTION.

You eagerly open the door and there in the center of the room is an image of you as a child laughing and giggling and emitting a wonderful energy of lightness. And then, it is up to you to bring into this room all the people in your life you associate with times of joy, from your early childhood to the present time. And each person who comes in gives you a big, loving hug and with each new person, the atmosphere becomes more light and bouncy. If anyone comes into the room with a solemn expression, just ask them if they are in the right room and give them a gentle kick!

Stay within this room as long as you like, feeling the energy of love and joy fill your whole being, feeling its warmth, knowing that this is your birthright, that you can create this sensation in your life in the present and well into the future. Also, feel the energy within this room run through your veins, healing your body and mind.

Finally, in your own time, take your leave from this room but carry with you that feeling of lightness, knowing that you can return there any time you want.

And then, walk back along and out of the corridor, slowly return to your body, and open your eyes.

Fear

Fear is the very antithesis of feeling your own strength, that source of the Healer Within, because if you fear something, you immediately give it power over you.

This is how epidemics gain momentum, whether it is 'flu, the bubonic plague or AIDS. Of course, there is the physical virus in the first place, but once a virus is seen as all-pervading, then the spectre of this tiny virus becomes lodged in people's minds as a threat of immense proportions. Take a minor disease like 'flu for example. How many times have you heard people say: 'I always seem to get 'flu at this time of the year' or 'Have you heard? There's a new strain of 'flu virus around'? Words, as I shall demonstrate later, are powerful things – in putting such thoughts into words, or even harboring suppressed fear that such thoughts engender, you are putting energy into that entity we call 'flu, cancer, or AIDS. Even by giving it a name, we give it an identity, a power of its own.

This may run counter to the rational way in which you have been taught cause and effect, but just think back on your life how fears have often become reality. Fear is an intangible force which governs the lives of so many people.

Fear manifests itself in many ways and is essentially a product of the rational mind. The one thing that I will always tell people, whether healthy or sick, is to learn to distinguish that inner voice of true intuition from the voice

106

of fear – over the next few weeks, just try this out.

Throughout our lives, we are confronted with many choices, and it is through the way we make these choices that we determine the direction of our lives: the ease or pain of our lives depends on these choices.

Sometimes, these present themselves as a clear cut decision between two opposites, yet, just as frequent, but less recognized, are those little flashes of inspiration that come through our mind just to do something because it feels right. And how often we dismiss such thoughts from our mind, because they are just 'too unconventional' or because the risks of following such a path seem too great.

This is why I say that fear is a product of the rational mind. Our intuition is that part of us which is in touch with the whole picture, whilst our rational mind is what divides everything into little parcels, separating this aspect of life from that. Our rational mind will always see reasons why we should not do things: i.e. the risks are too great; what other people will think; things are bad, but better the devil you know than the devil you don't know – and then, before you know it, fear sets in, paralyzes you and your intuitive feeling is swamped.

In letting fear smother your intuition, you are turning away from your true self, your highest creativity. In the end, it is the law of the Universe that something will stop you short and make you think and learn and understand how you are running away from your essence. And the way in which we confront this challenge is a symbol of the way we confront our selves. If we learn and follow our intuition and leave our fear and the past behind, focusing on our present being and true potential, then we can also leave behind whatever is blocking our path.

If you fear something, this means you do not understand the metaphysical truth behind it. If something is blocking your way, it is there for a reason. If you fear it, you give it power over you; if you are willing to learn from it and understand why it is blocking your way, it will eventually dissolve.

How often in the past have I banged my head against an obstacle in my life when all it needed for it to disappear was for it to teach me a simple lesson. Nowadays, it is the common cold which always gives me the message that I am allowing something to have power over me because I am acting through fear or am not trusting my own intuition. I get a cold, which will stay with me until I recognize and let go of what I am allowing to obstruct my path; when I do let go, the cold and the obstacle disappear simultaneously and almost instantly.

A life-threatening disease such as cancer or AIDS is an infinitely more powerful message. Yet, if you go deep within yourself and peel away all those layers of fear, of pain and of surrendering your own power, it is an even more powerful vehicle for change. When you have reached that essence within, that trust in yourself, then the balance within you will be naturally restored and your body will quite simply take care of itself.

To understand this means you must listen to your intuition and feel what is right. To put it into effect needs patience, for patience is trusting that something will happen in its own time; impatience, looking for an instant cure, is fearing deep down that it will not happen.

Fear of Intimacy

One of the most common fears that I find in people is the fear of intimacy, something I touch on in the chapter on isolation.

Fear of intimacy is in reality a combination of many fears: it is the fear of being let down, hurt or rejected or making a fool of yourself; it is a lack of self-confidence; it is fear of opening up to another person the parts of yourself you have buried deepest, as this also means that you have to confront them yourself; it is fear of showing your own vulnerability, even the fear of showing parts of yourself of which you are secretly ashamed. But, the root of it all is simply the fear of letting go, following your intuition and putting your trust in another person.

And the reasons behind this fear are just as diverse: there may have been a particularly bad experience in the past upon which you judge other people; a parent or a person of authority may have told you never to trust anyone or that you should always keep a part of you secret; within men in particular, there is the ridiculous social pressure of equating 'masculinity' with not showing your feelings. The list is endless . . . and sad.

For intimacy is the truest expression of your highest self, of that loving part of you. It is also the essence of balance: of giving and receiving equally.

And once more, the only guide to the degree you open up to another person is your intuition. Everybody has that gut feeling – not to be confused with a sexual feeling! – when we meet someone with whom we feel particularly comfortable and in tune, yet how many of us have the courage to follow this up and allow a relationship, at whatever level, to develop in its own way?

And, when I talk about intimacy, I do not mean the tendency of certain people to be open and smiling and friendly to everyone they meet, yet for whom, beneath this superficial geniality, the barriers to true intimacy are even thicker. You can fool others but, in the end, you cannot fool your body. Be honest with yourself and be aware of the depth of intimacy to which you are prepared to go.

For this is the message I wish to get over, as I shall more forcibly in the chapter on love. Only if you are able to open your heart and truly express your inner self will the Healer Within be fully activated; if you turn away from this, you turn away from your source of inner strength.

Which bring me to one final, very specific fear.

The Fear of Getting Well
Your first reaction to seeing this heading may well be: 'How sick! How can anyone be afraid of getting better?'

My answer to that is this: think back to what I have already written about the emptiness within a person giving space for the consciousness of dis-ease to enter and you may begin to

109

see a stumbling block that may confront certain people who are critically ill or even those in emotional turmoil.

For many of us, dis-ease, on whatever level, has proven to be a great impetus for inner growth and change. However, in going through the various stages of growth, there is always the memory within us of what life used to be like before this dis-ease came along and shoved us in the right direction. Often, the memory is of a way of life that seemed to lack any sense of direction and inner fulfillment.

So, lurking deep in the recesses of our minds, there may be that nagging question: 'If I attain that ultimate goal and rid myself of this dis-ease, may I not then return to the emptiness and lack of purpose that was in my life before I got sick?' It sounds like an unlikely question, but it is not uncommon.

It is a very easy mistake to make: associating the growth that one has undergone with the dis-ease itself, as opposed to seeing that the dis-ease was purely a means of initiating that growth. Instead of appreciating that one has directed one's own growth and that this growth will continue, one sees it as beginning and ending with the dis-ease. It is also as if the dis-ease has become a familiar friend without whom one is afraid to go out at night!

So, when I write about the fear of getting well, I really mean the fear of returning to the past and the fear of facing a future without the familiarity of something to hold on to. But, of course, no one ever returns to the past after such a period of intense change unless they make a very conscious decision to do so and the future takes care of itself if we live in the eternal present and follow our intuition.

Indeed, this particular fear shows what lies at the very heart of the emotion of fear: a sense of one's own limitation, the feeling that we are at the mercy of 'cruel fate' and that we are not able to or are not worthy of creating whatever reality we truly desire – which is why it is so important to understand what creativity really means.

Creativity and Limitation

So, what do I really mean by creativity? To most people, the word conjures up the image of some artistic talent, which is indeed part of it. Yet, creativity is something much broader than this. It is, as the word says, the ability to create one's own reality – *from within*.

What is the essence of creativity in an artistic sense? Quite simply, it is, to begin with, recognizing a particular ability and then giving it free expression. How many of us see great actors, musicians, painters etc. and wish we had their talent, or, more to the point, wish we had a particular talent through which we could express that inner part of ourselves?

The truth is, of course, that we all have an incredible well of creativity within us – every single one of you reading this book. It may not be something that leads to fame, such as the talents mentioned above, – and who needs fame anyway? – but we all have something within us that is special to ourselves, which is there just waiting to be released and freely expressed. It may be as a carpenter, a designer, a gardener or a technician; it may be as a teacher, an adviser and comforter of other people, a special knack with children or the elderly – the diversity of man is infinite.

For many of us, it takes a long time for us to recognize where this special creativity within us truly lies. From early childhood, we are constantly bombarded by those things we

111

'ought' to do through the expectations of our parents and family, but this more often than not has more to do with conformity and earning a living than true creativity. And, of course, as we grow older, most of us bend to the will and collective pressure of the so-called 'standards' of society.

It often takes a major upset in our lives for us to really confront and accept our true creativity. How many of us have settled into a comfortable routine existence, accepting second best, instead of actively going out and fulfilling that creative side of us?

Well, dis-ease, whether the reality or the fear of it, can be the most gigantic vehicle to unleash that creativity within you. It has brought you to a stop to face yourself – not the picture you offer to the world, not just the parts of you that you choose to acknowledge, not just you as a career person, a lover, a parent, but as a whole, complete being. And, within that whole, is your every essence, the true expression of your very individual self.

MEDITATION NO.5

As before, you center yourself and enter into the corridor which is your second chakra. You walk to the end of the corridor into a room marked CREATIVITY.

As you shut the door behind you and turn to the center of the room, you create in front of you an image of yourself in whatever you feel to be your most creative guise, whether as a teacher, actor, carpenter, counsellor etc., even as a parent or a lover. As you do so, you become that figure and feel what it is like inside you when you express that creative part of you.

Then, as you are expressing this creative instinct within you – and it does not have to be just one – somebody out of your past comes up and tells you that you are actually not creative in this way. This

opens the floodgates and, one by one, all those people who have tried to turn you away from your creativity and have tried to impose limitation upon you come up to you.

As each one comes before you and you listen to their judgment of you, you take them by the hand and say: 'I thank you for your opinion of me and what you think is right for me. However, this is only your view of me, of what perhaps you want me to be. It has nothing to do with who I really am.' You release them, let them stand to one side and allow the next to come before you: parents who wanted something for you which was not really you; teachers who said you were not good enough; peers who dismissed your idea of creativity as inferior to theirs; the countless people who have tried to impose their limited vision of reality upon you.

Finally, you bring in front of yourself that figure which is you, for you have surely at times during your life put limitations on your creativity, saying: 'Oh no! I'm not capable of that!' And, just as with all the others, you take this figure by the hand and release it too.

When you have done this, you line up all these people, and you blow a whistle. From the depths of the room, a train comes chugging in – it is marked: *Expresstrain to Limitation.* All these people climb on board, you give another whistle and the train chugs out of the room, into the corridor and out into the distance. So, now, you are left alone in this room and within this new space, you can create your own reality. You affirm and see in this room the reality you wish to create – not just the outward trappings of your creative guise, but your ability to bring into your life what you want and know you deserve, from health and fitness to warm relationships and prosperity.

Finally, when you are satisfied that you have covered all you need to, you leave this room of creativity, knowing that this is your birthright and you return to your body.

The Third Chaka: the Seat of the Ego

As I briefly mentioned in an earlier chapter, the third chakra often seems to be the most difficult to comprehend and it is therefore no coincidence that it is in this center that most of us get really stuck. We can easily relate to such notions as emotions, sex, love, communication, but the concepts of ego, power and strength are less clear to us.

One of the reasons why this is the case is that these issues are rarely confronted in our Western world, largely because ego and power are the driving forces behind our culture and are accepted as being an integral part of our lives.

Power versus strength, ego and pride versus faith and trust; these are the primeval conflicts which are the hallmark of our modern world. Ever since man became a 'conscious' being, aware of his differences from other men and forms of life, this conflict has been working itself out on every single level of our existence, from the personal and individual to the political and global.

National and international conflict is such an integral part of history books, going as far back as the Old Testament and ancient mythology, that we accept it as a necessary evil. As long as it does not come too close to home, we take in the pictures on television of this act of terrorism or that war in a far off land, but we have by now become immune to their effect.

What most of us do not understand, though, is that these

115

conflicts on a global level are merely a reflection of what is occurring within the narrower plane of our own lives. For thousands of years, now, our planet earth has been the seat of power and ego within our solar system, and only when this is worked out on the individual level in the personal lives of the millions of people on earth will this final conflict be fully resolved.

You may well believe that writing in such terms is a little unrealistic and I am in no way suggesting that this transformation will happen overnight. But I do not need to tell you about the pace of change which is taking place within people's lives at this period in time – you would not be reading this book if this were not the case in your own life.

Our planet earth is at present at the third chakra level within our solar system, and what this so-called 'New Age' is all about is the gradual shifting of energy and raising of vibration from this plane to the level of the heart, the fourth chakra. This is why we are all going through such an intense time in our personal lives at this time: we ourselves are being prepared to accept this higher vibration into our being, so that we can in turn help to open up others to create the domino effect of change on a heart level rather than the customary level of power.

Now, if you are going through a particularly tough time at this moment, your thoughts will be turned within yourself, far away from creating the change within others. But, this does not matter. It is your willingness to change and grow which raises the vibration around you and affects the energy of others around you, even though you may not be aware of this.

Whatever pain or emotional turmoil you are going through at this moment, there is light at the end of the tunnel and this light is the light of your feeling and understanding of your connection to your higher self and ultimately to the Universe itself.

What blocks that light is your ego.

So what is the meaning of this word, ego, which everyone seems to be using so much nowadays.

In our current language, we associate it with the word egotism with all its connotations of selfishness and arrogance, yet ego goes far beyond this.

Ego is strongly attached to the rational side of our nature. It has, over the period of our evolution, driven us forward in the search for knowledge and for a better material existence. Yet, when it is not balanced by the intuitive, spiritual part of our nature, the ego leads us away from the natural harmony of a world built on love and compassion.

The fundamental nature of ego is separateness from God. It is the opposite of faith because it denies our ability to draw upon the Energy of the Whole, the Universe.

Ego has to do with power. On the one hand, there is the way in which we all to varying degrees put out our power, using control, manipulation, possessiveness, judgment etc. as an integral part of our life.

On the other side of the coin, there is the way in which we relinquish the power we have over our own lives and submit to the views of others.

These two supposed opposites are by no means mutually exclusive. As I will show you in an example later on, the one can actually feed the other, continuously jumping backwards and forwards from one end of the spectrum to the other.

Ego is also need – in not feeling our connection to the Universe, we always feel the need to search for something to attach ourselves to. It is that compulsive desire to see things and in particular people in relation to ourselves rather than as entities in their own right. Material ambition and competitiveness are each forms of this need, just as envy and jealousy are results of this mentality.

Certainly, ego is arrogance and pride, but it is also that part of us which puts ourselves down and says that we are not worthy or good enough.

More than anything, when we are talking about the Healer Within, all activity of the ego, from possessiveness to judgment, competitiveness to an inferiority complex, means that you are putting your energy out in a totally uncreative way. It means that you are trying to control and make everything into a struggle rather than trusting your intuition to guide you in all the major decisions of your life. There is an inner tension and stress behind all behavior related to the ego – remember what I wrote about the relationship between the third chakra and the adrenal glands at the beginning of this book.

What I am asking you to do in the next few chapters is to really examine within yourself the extent to which the ego part of you governs your actions. Without exception, every single person with whom I have worked over the years has had some degree of imbalance in the third chakra related to ego and it is hardly surprising. This ego part of us, which in many ways has contributed to our evolution and growth, is also the final obstacle that we all have to confront on the path to our higher selves.

Control

When I mentioned power just now, I referred to the two supposed ends of the spectrum: putting one's power out in terms of control and manipulation, and giving up one's own power by allowing oneself to be controlled. In reality, the one has a great deal to do with the other, and this inter-relationship, this swinging between the one and the other, is very important when we are looking at any imbalance within all of us.

Let me illustrate this with an example of a person whom I shall call John.

I went to see John at the request of a friend of his. John had been seriously ill for just over a year.

Before becoming sick, his was outwardly the perfect existence. He had a very successful, albeit high-pressured career, which earned him a lot of money. He had a beautiful apartment, travelled a lot between America and Europe, was considered very attractive, easy going, with lots of friends and seemingly no problems whatsoever. On the surface, he had the ideal existence.

Yet, when I went to see him, the dead weight that I felt emanating from the area of this third chakra was heavier than anything I had ever felt before.

The story behind it all was this.

John's father had been, until his retirement, an extremely successful, aggressive, self-made businessman. Although, as

119

he grew up, John was emotionally closer to his mother, there was the continuing pressure from his father, often unspoken, to go out and make a career for himself. Without really taking into account what his son wanted, the father made certain openings for him which would allow him to start on the path towards success. Sure enough, driven by the desire to prove himself coupled with an innate intelligence, John became successful very quickly. The fact that he had wanted to go to university and have a spell of freedom rather than embark on a career straight from school was soon forgotten.

That was the first stage. Having reached this level of success, where did he go from there? From time to time, he would wonder where it all led and what the point of it all was, but such doubts were soon swept under the carpet. He had thought how nice it would be to take a year off, but the figure of his father still loomed in the background.

As time went by, he developed a great social life, lots of acquaintances, wild parties and the drugs that went with them. He had no problem meeting people for sex, but, as far as relationships were concerned, he always seemed to end up with people who were rather domineering and were incapable of showing any warmth: almost a reflection of his outer self. His friends were not the kind of people he could relate too deeply to; they tended to be drawn to the image of perfect control which he projected, and, in the end, he grew to like the idea of having this 'circle' around him.

So, with all of this going for him, why did he end up getting sick? It has all to do with Control.

From the very instant that he made the decision to follow his father's vision of him rather than his own, he started on a merry-go-round which became faster and faster and increasingly more difficult to get off. From the feeling of having to prove himself and get approval from others, of always having to do better, came that drive to control every aspect of his life, to structure and plan his existence around a goal that he did not fully understand. When he was away from this treadmill, he reckoned he deserved the pleasure of going to the other extreme of going wild and losing control.

And, as he became more and more an image of success in other people's eyes, he gradually came to see his life through their eyes. Every so often, deep down, he would feel an inner yearning for something simpler and more meaningful, but, by then, he could not let the mask of control fall.

For that is what it had become: a mask of control. He always had to maintain an image, the hard shell over a void of emptiness, the need to control for fear of losing control. During the day, he was the model of self-control, the successful businessman, being able to handle and manipulate any situation; during the night, the pent-up tension was released in a frenzy of constant activity.

In relationships, the reason he always attracted the same kind of person was that this seemed the one way to relinquish this control. In the quiet of a 'private' life, he wanted the very opposite of his 'public' life – he wanted someone to take over control, but constantly confused the giving and receiving of a warm, loving relationship with the projection he made of someone who would be dominant and taken any responsibility of the relationship away from him. He was often left hurt and with the feeling of being used by such people.

When I first went to see him, he was polite, but saw my visit as an intrusion. I worked with him once and then, when I was working with him during my second visit, there was a reaction like an exploding gun, an anger directed towards me with a vehemence I had never before experienced: what had I done to deserve to be so healthy, when he who had done no wrong was sick? It all poured out and eventually turned to tears; he finally expressed his true feelings of sadness that people had never really loved him for who he was, and of fear that, if he did get better, he would return to that sense of emptiness that had gnawed away inside him for years before.

In the end, he did die, but only after he had found a certain peace within himself, making peace with and expressing his feelings to his family and friends. He died because, deep down, he made the choice, believing that this was the only way not to have to struggle any more. I respect his choice, although dying is by no means the only way to rise above having to struggle and keep a controlling grip on life.

I have spent so long describing this somewhat extreme case, because there are elements within this story which apply in varying degrees to many people I have seen.

The essence of this story is: *not being true to oneself.*

This can be manifested in so many ways: being constantly influenced and worried by other people's opinions, or making decisions because they follow the route of conformity rather than an individual gut feeling, are but a couple of examples. Fundamentally, it is a matter of consciously or subconsciously giving up your power to other people or to outside forces.

At the beginning, it is a process that can easily be reversed, but, as time goes by, such behavior can become so ingrained that one's true desires and creativity become relegated to the deep recesses of the subconscious. The gulf between one's inner aspirations and the outer mask is not just symbolic; as this gulf becomes wider, a very real and ever growing emptiness develops between them, a void which allows a consciousness such as cancer, AIDS or any major disease to enter within. And, to make matters worse, those who have developed this mask are the first to fool themselves and others into believing that there is nothing lacking inside. I have lost count of those who have angrily denied any such lack when I have first pointed it out to them, only for them to admit to it later on.

It all goes back to the chapter on creativity. When we ignore our true creativity, our inner selves, we are literally turning our backs on ourselves, our inner strength. This leads in turn to a suppression of other aspects of our lives – our emotions, our true feelings and aspirations – until a lingering sense of dissatisfaction and lack of fulfilment becomes almost accepted as something which must be born in life: the philosophy of 'You can't have your cake and eat it.'

In the case I have just illustrated, a seemingly ideal existence concealed a deep-felt emptiness, and the control needed to hide this void from other people literally tore his mind and body apart. His was certainly the most extreme case of this that I have encountered, yet it would do no harm for all of us to look closely at ourselves and see to what extent we have surrendered our power to others and buried our true selves and aspirations under the superficial goals which our society rates so highly.

MEDITATION NO.6

As with the previous few meditations, you center yourself, come out of your body and, this time, face your third chakra at your solar plexus. Again, you see a corridor stretch out in front of you and you walk along this until you come to a door marked AUTHORITY FIGURES.

As you walk into the room behind the door, you prepare yourself to bring in front of you all those people and entities that you have at some point in your life allowed to have power over you.

First of all, you bring in front of you your parents. They appear before you, you take them both by the hand, and, as you do so, the image of them is transformed. Suddenly, they are standing in front of you, completely naked and alone. You see them for what they are – two people whose lives, like yours, have been a succession of experiences, good and bad, and who are just what they are. They are neither perfect nor totally bad. They just are, and, as you see them naked in front of you, you know that they can have no power over you. For once and for all, you release any sense that you must live your life according to their values.

123

Likewise, you bring into your presence any other members of your family and have them stand naked in front of you, releasing any hold they have over you.

Then, you bring into your presence other stereo-typical authority figures, such as teachers, priests, and, in particular, doctors. And they stand before you, naked and alone, human beings like yourself with their own ups and downs in their personal lives. Their views may be right for their own lives, but have no hold over yours. You know that they are passing on to you only their personal view of reality and that their pronouncements have no power over you.

Then, you bring into your presence all those at work or in other spheres of your life who seem to have some measure of control over your life, and you take them by the hand and their clothes just fall off them, leaving these naked figures in front of you, which can have no power over you. You do not judge them; you accept them as they are and let them go.

Next, you bring before you all those people you consider to be more powerful than you – people who seem to be more successful, more attractive, whose lives seem to be easier or more exciting, everybody you look up to. Again, you take them by the hand and they appear naked in front of you, neither greater nor smaller than you, and you realise that comparison is worthless. They are what they are; you are what you are, no less creative than them, only creative in your own individual way.

Once you have gone through all individuals you know who have exerted some power over you, you turn to other symbols of authority. You bring before you a certain type of person you try and emulate, or the symbol of the kind of society you have felt you must conform to. When you take them by the hand, they too stand naked and helpless in front of you, neither more nor less powerful than you – just different.

Likewise, you bring forward those people or symbols who have judged you for what you are and, as they stand naked before you, you see that they have no power, let alone right, to impose their personal views upon you.

Moving forward even from symbols, you visualize objects, entities or abstract ideas which you have allowed to hold sway over you.

First, you see a specific disease in front of you and see it as a microscopic virus. You put out your hand to touch it, and, as you do so, it disintegrates. You reclaim your power and know that no such tiny organism can have power over you.

In the same way, you see drugs or alcohol or any other substance which you have allowed to have power over you. You put out your hand to touch them and see them disintegrate before your eyes. And you understand that you do not need them any longer.

Then, you bring into your presence anything that seems to stand in your way. If you are always short of money, you see a pile of bills in front of you; you reach out and touch them and they too disintegrate, so that you know that they too have no power over you and that you can create your own material prosperity. And you do likewise with anything else that blocks your way. You put your hand out with faith and see it disintegrate as it has no power over you.

Finally, you stand in this room and look around at all the naked figures surrounding you. You see that not one of them has any kind of authority over you; as you look at them, naked, exactly as they are, you take a deep breath and reclaim mastery over your own life, responsibility for your own decisions and actions.

Then, in your own time, you leave this room, walk out of your third chakra and back into your body.

Judgment and Guilt

Just think how many times in a day you judge other people, even your closest friends, and, of course, yourself. Judgment is all to do with power and comparison, nothing to do with inner strength.

In the case of self-judgment, it is again a matter of surrendering your own power. How many of us feel that we are not physically attractive, not too bright or amusing or interesting, and how often do we allow this to filter down to a deeper judgment of ourselves and see ourselves as inferior beings compared with other people around us? It is this self-judgement which robs us of the feeling of our own self-worth and this ultimately leads us to believe that we have no power to create what we really want in our lives.

Judgment is an extension of ego. It is that part of us which must always see ourselves in comparison with other people and which constantly plays games, sometimes putting us on a pedestal, sometimes putting us down. Instead of being at peace with ourselves, there is the constant need to compare our state of being with others, as if this were the only way of judging our own self-worth.

The more we build up expectations of ourselves and of other people, the more we judge when these expectations are not met. As soon as we build up an expectation of somebody, we are putting them into a strait-jacket of our own making – we are basically seeing this person as a projection of ourselves

126

rather than as the individual that he or she is.

The act of judgment is basically an act of intolerance. It gives power to that part of you which says that what is right for you is right for everybody, rather than understanding that everyone has the right to act in their own way and create their own reality.

Indeed, judgement betrays an inability to see deep within yourself as much as an unwillingness to relate deeply to others. Just for a moment think of the person you judge most, who irritates you most. Then, think of what it is about this person which you judge most of all and try to understand how this relates to you. The reason I ask you to do this is that, when we judge a particular aspect of another person's character or behavior, it is because this is a reflection of an aspect within our own character or behavior that we like least of all. When I was first told this, my first reaction was one of ridicule, but, once I was honest with myself and looked really deeply at my own behavior. I understood how very true this was.

I mentioned in the chapter on forgiveness how much more difficult it can be to forgive oneself than to forgive others, and this leads on to this most destructive and most pointless of emotions: guilt.

'Don't be so hard on yourself!' How often have you heard that said? In this modern world, where we are brought up to achieve, to reach the highest standards (whatever they are supposed to be), how common it is to see people driving themselves crazy to meet a set of goals that have little to do with their inner selves, but are merely imposed upon them by pressure from parents, peer groups or society in general. The pressure to conform is enormous and failure to live up to certain so-called 'standards' results in one or both of the two main forms of guilt: self-judgement or assumption of other people's judgment.

In many ways, these two are one and the same thing. When I say assumption of other people's judgment, what I mean is the way in which we are constantly bombarded by the judgment of others over some aspect of our behavior to such a degree that we come to assume a feeling of guilt over it. Self-judgement of course comes from the same source, but, for many, self-judgment itself is an addictive pattern, born from a need, instilled from an early age, to constantly prove oneself, to perform above the standards of others.

In addition to this, there is the traditional, moralistic view of so-called right and wrong, the rigidity of which runs counter to the whole concept of the Healer Within. In fact, the belief that there is one set of values applicable to the whole diversity of mankind living on this planet is presumptuous to say the least. Anyone who has traveled around the world cannot help noticing that attitudes and behavior are formed by the social, climatic and many other conditions particular to a certain area; no one means of social living is superior or inferior to another, as each evolves in its own manner.

I am always somewhat distrustful of the type of person who is always claiming to be 'objective'. As far as I am concerned, there is no such thing as objectivity, as we are all influenced by the subjective impressions which are constantly forming us throughout our lives. For example, the way that your mother sees you is completely different from the way that someone at work sees you, which is completely different from the way you see yourself – and yet, you are still the same person.

All the basic laws of behavior which exist in most societies, such as 'Thou shalt not kill', are those which are necessary in group living and which fundamentally prevent an individual from invading another person's space. The so-called 'moral majority' and any individual who presumes to tell another person how he or she should live are, in effect, doing just that: invading another person's space. In the name of 'morality', they are wanting to impose a rigid structure of their own choosing upon society and are actually destroying the natural flow which exists in the evolution of our species.

All of us are brought up with certain belief systems inherited from our close family, and yet, for us to create our own reality, we must examine these as we go through our lives and learn to feel whether they still ring true for us. If they do not, then we must trust that feeling.

Guilt basically arises from a lack of trust and faith in your own feelings and actions. Guilt attaches itself to that part of you which has been told or subconsciously believes that a certain aspect of your behavior is wrong. Guilt is the most powerfully destructive emotion because it creates a revolving circle from which it becomes more and more difficult to escape.

Of course, all of us make mistakes, do things we regret and even consciously hurt other people, but, in the end, for most of us, our conscience is our guide. If we do something we later regret, it is that sentient part of us which makes us feel remorse. Remorse is the trigger which makes us learn from our actions, while guilt is the act of holding on to this feeling of remorse.

If we do something which *we ourselves* feel was wrong, our conscience tells us so and, in the world of the Healer Within, we look at ourselves and learn what made us act in this way, so that we need not repeat the same behavior. In the world of guilt, we do not accept this as a lesson, but beat our breast and carry the sense of remorse around with us. And, more than likely, we shall end up doing exactly the same thing again!

Guilt is really a very self-indulgent emotion!

The fact is that there are no 'oughts' and 'shoulds' in this world. This is why guilt should never be confused with responsibility. Guilt is buying in to another person's or even your own illusion of what you 'ought' to be; responsibility is living in the present and continuously acting in a way which *you feel* is right.

It is important for you to occasionally take time to sit back and recognize that you are essentially a warm and loving being, especially if you are going through a period when you do not feel good about yourself and your life. It is the quality of your feelings that matters. What you feel deep within yourself is your true essence and to in any way judge that essence is one of the best ways to throw yourself out of balance.

Your essence is your strength; this strength and the balance it maintains within your body and spirit depends on your living according to your genuine feelings and your intuition, rather than submitting to the judgment of people who do not care to know what is truly going on within you. By turning against or in any way judging that emotional, individual part of you which is your own true self, you are turning away from your own source of inner strength.

That is why guilt, by smothering your life force, can quite literally kill.

MEDITATION NO.7

As before, close your eyes and focus on that central part of yourself and then move down to the area of your third chakra.

This time, you imagine yourself coming out of your body, shrinking down in size and facing your third chakra as if it is a long corridor stretching out in front of you. You enter this corridor and walk down until you come to a door, over which is marked the word: GUILT. You walk into a room and stand in the center.

What you are now going to do is bring into the room all those people who have imposed a feeling of guilt upon you, starting with your parents. See them standing in front of you and see how they have harbored expectations for you, and when you have 'disappointed' these expectations, notice how they have judged you and how you have assumed this mantle of judgment upon yourself. If this has never been the case with your parents, let this pass, but be aware of any instance that they have judged you.

Then, as they stand there in front of you, walk up to them, take them by the hand and say to them:

'I thank you for your opinion and your perception of me. What I do in my life is my responsibility and there are no "oughts" in this world. If I do something, it is I who take the consequences and I do not live my life through the eyes of others. Therefore, I release any judgment that you have imposed upon me and I act according to my own conscience. I feel no guilt for not living up to your expectations.'

From this point, you can bring before you any other people, even symbols such as a priest or the press, and repeat the same process, letting go of the hold which each of them has over you.

Then, bring in front of you any people towards whom you feel guilty because of any hurt you may have caused them. Ask their forgiveness and feel the release of accepting this from them, as they take your hands and let go of the emotional charge between you.

Finally, bring a mirror image of yourself in front of you and ask the question: 'What aspects of your life, your behavior, your character do you like least about yourself? Why is is that you judge this part of yourself?'

And, as you see yourself in these roles, you say to yourself: 'I forgive myself for behaving in this way and I no longer judge myself. If I repeat this behaviour, I shall not be harsh upon myself, but shall be aware of my actions, understand and let them go, until I no longer need to repeat these patterns of behavior.'

Finally, say to yourself: 'I do not deserve to be sick. Whatever may have caused imbalance within my body in the past I now release from me and I see myself as being worthy of a healthy and fulfilling life.'

As you stand in this room, you see all those people you summoned into the room, including the image of yourself, file out through the door, until you are left alone.

As you breath in the space of this room, you assert to yourself: 'I shall never again allow the feeling of guilt to enter my being. I shall act according to my own conscience and not allow the views of others to dictate my behavior. I trust myself and know that I shall grow from any mistakes I make.'

With this assertion of your own inner strength and guidance, walk out of the room, along the corridor and gradually return to your own body and space.

Addiction and Isolation

Nowhere is the effect of guilt more deadly than when we are concerned with addictive behavior.

No addiction just arises of itself. There are experiences and conditions within our lives which lead us into repeating the same behavior over and over again, of looking for a way to escape, however temporarily, from the reality around us, from the emptiness of our inner lives. Guilt is the best way to perpetuate such a condition.

The more we judge ourselves for behaving in an addictive manner and the harder we are on ourselves for each 'lapse', the more our self-esteem will slip and the more addictive the pattern will become. This is the way guilt works, for it puts energy into the object of its fury and, in doing so, gives it power over us, binding us even closer to our addictive behavior.

Now, it may be that there is a little voice within you saying: 'It is something we should feel bad about. We all know that no good can come of it.' If you assume such a position, you have not learned the lesson of forgiving yourself and letting go. If you want to break a habit of any kind, the first step is to accept what was done in the past as being firmly locked up in the past without blame, without being harsh upon yourself. If you wish to change, you will do so in time by understanding the root of your behavior, letting go of the judgment and allowing your self-esteem to return. If you continue to play the role of the 'Lady of Perpetual Guilt', you will quite simply remain stuck in the condition you are trying to escape.

A couple of pages back, I touched on the emptiness which all of us have felt at some point in our lives: an emptiness which cannot be filled by a good job, a nice house, 'sex, drugs, rock 'n' roll', outer possessions or fleeting pleasures.

Yet, sadly, it is with these very things that we try to fill the void that we sometimes feel within us. Of course, most people tend to think of addiction in terms of drugs, cigarettes or alcohol, but addictions go far beyond this to include sex, food, work, status, clothes – indeed, any material thing which will help to escape the need to delve deeply within oneself. There are not too many people who have no form of addiction whatsoever in their lives.

It is actually quite irrelevant what kind of addiction we have in our day to day lives. What is important is the source of this addiction, or, to put it another way, what is this void within us which we feel compelled to run away from?

Throughout this book, I have been focusing on the spiritual side of our nature and how only by recognizing it can we integrate the totality of our selves into our lives. Most of us, though, have been brought up in a society so obsessed by material values that we are led to believe that there is nothing beyond them which is important. We must strive to make a living which will enable us to live in comfort and security and even our human relationships are bound within certain limitations of wealth and education.

There comes a point, however, when we know within ourselves that this is just not enough. We become tired of superficial conversation. We know that there is something deeper within ourselves and we yearn to be able to share this with other people. If we feel that we cannot do so, we start to feel isolated, alienated and out of tune with the world.

Whether you live in a big city or a small close-knit community, the effect of this sense of isolation can gradually become devastating. In an urban environment, one can be surrounded by many acquaintances and yet still feel lonely; in a small community, one can feel stifled by the narrowness and claustrophobic nature of people's lives and views.

However, wherever one is, the truth is that it is a matter of personal choice whether or not we become isolated and feel out of synch with the world. It is no use feeling pity for oneself and escaping into drugs, alcohol etc., for these will feed the sense of isolation and then the journey back will be all the more difficult.

I have seen again and again, especially in big cities, people who are very social, always going out and doing things, seeing lots of people, flitting from one group to another, yet who have no real close friends when it comes down to the crunch. The way in which their lives are always filled with outer things to do is in itself an addiction, as this constant activity is merely a way of not having to confront their inner loneliness. But then, what happens when they are sitting alone at home and want to share their inner thoughts with someone? Where is there to turn during a crisis or if they get sick?

This is the kind of isolation which can really eat away at the very heart of someone, creating an emptiness which can allow all sorts of manifestations of imbalance to occur, such as deep depressions, addictions and ultimately sickness. And how ironic it is that those who feel the deepest sense of isolation are often those who, to the outside world, appear the least so, as they have perfected the mask of self-assurance so well.

In the end, though, if you wear a mask which is not your true self, then the only person you are fooling is yourself.

I know that there are certain rare individuals who choose a life or at least a period of isolation to focus on their inner selves, but they are few. For the majority, take away our fellow men and women and life loses its purpose. We are here to relate to each other, to learn from each other, to have fun with each other. It is people who offer the variety and energy of life – we only get out of human relationships what we put into them.

This balance of giving and receiving is the key, but then there is of course fear. Shyness is a form of fear – maybe a general lack of confidence, fear of rejection, even of intimacy, of really opening up your true self to another. Yet, in giving into this fear, you are turning away from your innate ability to create one of the things you want most in life: harmonious and fulfilling relationships in which you can share your inner feelings with others.

The question is: do you want to play games with people or do you wish to relate to them? I have so often heard people say that they feel out of tune with the world, but, if you project an image which is not truly you, how do you expect to attract towards you people who appreciate you as you truly are?

It is all a question of openness and of understanding that you deserve the highest and most fulfilling relationships. If you remain closed and convinced that you are not worthy, of course people will pick this up and stay away from you. If you are open and trust your intuitive reaction towards people, the people of your energy will be drawn towards you. It is one of the simple laws of the Universe. Like attract like.

On the other hand, if you present a false picture of yourself to others, those who are attracted towards you will be attracted towards this image rather than your true self and it is therefore likely that you will be unable to relate to them on a deep level.

It is, as I said, a matter of choice.

When we are talking about addiction, the choice is the same. The only difference is that, with drug addiction as an example, that choice becomes more difficult to make as one becomes more and more deeply enmeshed in the addictive cycle.

As someone who has tried a few of the 'lighter' recreational drugs, I find it very easy to see how any drug can become addictive, for, like no other substance, do they take you on a high far away from 'reality'. They seem to be quite simply a wonderful temporary escape from day to day existence. And, needless to say, when people start taking them, they never think in terms of addiction.

But, for many people, these short term escapes into a realm of no cares begin to appear to be the only way out from the 'sordid reality' and drudgery of their day to day existence. From that point on, addiction is assured: there is the agonizing depression of coming down from a high, which makes 'reality' seem worse and worse and the desire to escape it stronger and stronger.

You will note that the word 'reality' keeps popping up again and again, and this is in many ways the key to the state of mind which allows addictive behavior to take hold. If we perceive the so-called real world as unjust or superficial and we feel out of tune with it, that same old feeling of isolation and emptiness starts creeping back into the picture again.

I know only too well from my own experience the confusion that can be felt when confronted by a society which seems to be obsessed with superficial and material things with no apparent concern for the more human, personal aspects of life. Yet, even if this reality seems to be unbearable and you try to escape it through drugs or whatever means, you are adding to the power of this 'real' world. You are quite simply saying: 'I do not like it. I can do nothing about it, so I will escape it as much as I can' – yet another example of turning away from your own strength and yielding power to the source of your discontent.

What increases the sense of isolation is the scorn which this same society heaps upon people who become addicted to drugs. It is the beginning of a vicious circle. First, the escape from a society whose values mean nothing to you, followed by the judgment of that society and increasingly compounded by a feeling of lack of self-worth.

Each of these stages on the downward spiral are tantamount to giving up your own source of inner strength, first by running away from the world and yourself, and then by seeing yourself as others see you, accepting that you do not deserve the best in your life. And, the more you surround yourself with other people who share this low view of themselves, the more this feeling of powerlessness will feed itself.

If your life seems full of hardship and you are constantly condemning the world as being unjust to you, then you are seeing yourself as a mere pawn in the game of life rather than drawing upon that inner reserve of energy to direct your own life. If, on the other hand, you confront this seeming injustice and understand that the only reality that faces you is the one you create, you can start to see yourself as you are: an individual in your own right who can build your own life on that nature within you which is special to you.

Strength and Faith

Compared with the constant activity of the ego, inner strength may seem somewhat boring, but, in reality, it is quite the opposite, as it opens one up to the endless possibilities of one's own creativity.

Just think back over your life and remember those few people you have encountered who radiate a wonderful sense of stillness and inner peace, for whom life appears to be so simple. They may not at first sight be the most lively and exciting people, but they give off an aura of quiet strength and trust which most of us would like to feel within ourselves.

Inner strength has nothing to do with power and ego. It just is. Inner strength is based on faith – it does not need to compare, because it knows that intuition and knowledge within are the only guides.

The essential work of the ego is to make us see our separateness, as opposed to our connection with this limitless Universe. It makes us see our achievements as arising solely from our own intellect and power; it tells us that we are alone in the world and must struggle for ourselves without expecting any help from outside – and when things go wrong, it is just cruel fate or chance. The ego sees faith as blind passivity, a substitute for those who are not bright or 'privileged' enough to think and act for themselves.

That ego part of us does not recognize that thinking,

acting and individuality are all essential to faith and inner strength.

The fact that we are all connected to that ultimate source of energy – the Universe, God, whatever you like to call it – does not mean that we immediately must surrender our individuality and become part of an amorphous mass. Nor does it mean that we have no responsibility and no power over our destiny. What it does mean is that we can tap into this source of limitless energy and potential and draw from it whenever we wish.

From the moment we are born, we are bombarded by a whole host of influences and patterns which mould us into the individual beings which we become. Unless we choose to surround ourselves with rigidity, this individuality is constantly changing as we perceive and continue to absorb all that happens around us.

As we grow older, we are confronted by more and more choices and possibilities. Every day, we have to make lots of minor decisions, but it is the major choices which determine the direction of our lives. We are only rarely confronted with these, but they invariably come at such particularly crucial points in our lives that we must always be open to act on and not walk away from such choices. The way we react to dis-ease is such a choice – on the level not only of physical health, but also of the way we take responsibility for the rest of our lives.

This is the essence of faith: knowing that we have the responsibility for the direction of our lives in our own hands and understanding that the path will be full of peace and joy if only we follow our intuition, our true nature.

It is only our ego which tells us otherwise. Our ego piles layer upon layer over this intuitive sense – as we get swept away following goals and behaving in ways that have little to do with our true nature and aspirations, we lose our intuitive connection with that Universal Energy. The road towards regaining that connection is by necessity one of patience, gradually peeling off layer after layer, letting go of all the excess baggage that you do not wish to carry

with you into the future, until you reach that inner core of yourself. Dis-ease is merely a stimulus for this change, and, like the rest of this excess, can also be left behind once this function is fulfilled.

MEDITIATION NO.8

Once again, center yourself, come out of your body and walk into this corridor which is your third chakra. As you walk along, you see on the walls seven barometers, each of them graded on a scale of zero to one hundred.

You walk up to the first one and you see the word POWER inscribed on it. As you stand before it, you look at your life and see how much you use power in your day to day dealings with people. How much do you manipulate and play games with other people? How possessive or jealous are you? How competitive or how ambitious for recognition and material goals are you? How rigidly do you try to control, structure and plan your life, rather than just following your intuition? How much do you judge others and, above all, yourself? On a scale of zero to one hundred, how do you think you rate in the power game? If you rate higher than you truly wish, then know that you can come back any time and see this barometer fall, by letting go of the *need* to continuously put out power and control.

You then leave this behind and walk up to the next barometer which is marked STRENGTH. How much of your life is based on inner strength rather than power? How much do you follow your inner voice rather than the opinions of others and of society? How much peace do you feel within yourself, rather than the need to be constantly going out and doing things? How much confidence do you have in your ability to create your own path in life, or do you still see yourself at the mercy of other people or of fate? From zero to one hundred, how strong are you within yourself?

The next barometer is COURAGE. How much do you stand up for what you feel is right, not just in the company of friends, but in all situations in your life? How much are you prepared to take your life by the scruff of its neck and follow your intuitive path, even if your rational side sees it as being too risky? How much are you prepared to run against the tide, be unconventional, as long as it feels right? How courageous are you, from zero to one hundred?

You then move on to COWARDICE. How often do you run away from things, especially your true self and the important choices you have to make? How often are you confronted with a choice and you take the easy option because it is less of a risk? How often do you shrink away from standing up for yourself or friends when you know that you or they are right? How much do you surrender your power to other people and live your life through their eyes rather than your own? How much do you surrender to fear? From zero to one hundred, how do you figure on the scale of cowardice?

The next barometer is HONESTY. How honest are you with other people? How truly do you express your emotions rather than bottling them up inside? How much do you hide from even your closest friends because you are ashamed of something in your life? And, just as important, how honest are you with yourself? How much do you play games with yourself, suppressing within you things that are important?

You then move on to TRUST. How much do you trust other people, or, more to the point, how much do you trust your intuitive feel for other people? How prepared are you to open yourself up to other people on a deep and meaningful level? Most important of all, how much to you trust your intuition? If you feel it is right to do something, do you just go ahead and do it? How much trust do you have in yourself as a divine being who can follow that higher self within you and create your own reality? How much do you trust in that Universal Energy to provide for you if you are prepared to put out to it what you really want?

The final barometer is PROSPERITY. Prosperity does not just mean material prosperity; it means that you are worthy of having in your life anything that you feel is right. How worthy do you think you are of having the highest and the best in your life? Do you put limitations upon yourself? Do you believe that you will have the highest and best relationship, no financial problems, no need to struggle in your life? Do you believe that you deserve to be perfectly healthy and therefore will be so? From zero to one hundred, how high is your prosperity consciousness?

You now leave these barometers behind, knowing that, at any time, you can return to them and move them up and down as you wish, knowing that it is purely up to you at what level they remain.

You then walk along the corridor until, right at the end, you come to a door which bears the inscription: STRENGTH. As you approach it, the door swings open of its own accord and there in front of you, glowing with a bright light, is the archetypal symbol of the Sword. It is hanging there in thin air and you know it is there for you. Although it is almost your size, you take it by the hilt and, as you lift it up above your head, it feels so light, yet full of energy. You practise swinging it around you and you know that this is the sword of your inner strength that you can draw upon at any time to cut through intolerance, through doubt, to sweep away anything that stands in the path towards your highest good. It is there for you, for you alone.

In your own time, you release this sword, once you feel comfortable with it, allowing it to hang there as it was before. You then turn and walk back towards the entrance to the corridor, knowing that you can return to pick up this sword of your own strength at any time.

Finally, you leave your third chakra behind, return to your own body and open your eyes.

The Fourth Chakra:
the Heart Center

The fourth chakra, the heart center, is often known as the 'Gateway to Heaven', because, in leaving the first three chakras behind, we are also leaving behind those aspects of ourselves which hold us back from our highest good. Only by understanding and letting go of all these outside forces which weigh us down can the true spirit within us rise up, grow and be freely expressed in our lives.

It has been necessary to painstakingly go through and identify all those 'lower' aspects of ourselves, for, if we still carry them on board, we cannot reach the higher elements within us – the strength and energy within is unable to be released to create the Healer Within.

For, remember, the heart center is the seat of the thymus, the regulator of the immune system. If this center is closed, so too is the thymus and the functioning of the immune system is impaired.

Throughout this book, I have been writing about our inner selves, the core of our existence and the deep sense of emptiness that many, consciously or subconsciously, feel within. Yet, I have only fleetingly touched on how we can expand that core within us to fill that void, that emptiness within.

Well, this will be the focus of the rest of this book, so that you may get a feel of what is your true source of strength, that essence within you which creates the foundation from which to build your own reality and, among other things, to heal yourself.

In a word, you could describe this essence as love.

But, of course, a word is just a word and, for many, the word 'love' has very wishy-washy or, at the other end of the spectrum, too specific connotations. Nearly every song you hear on the radio is about love in one way or another; there is the state of being 'in love' – there are endless variations within the feelings associated with the word. You may say you love your parents, your spouse or lover, your friends, your children, but the way you feel towards each of them is different.

Therefore, leave behind any preconceptions you have about love; we are going to strip away from it all but the barest essentials. We shall see that Love, in its truest form, has no boundaries and is the *highest form of spirit* that we can attain in our earthly form.

Man is both a physical and spiritual being. We are all living creatures in a physical form: we need food and water to survive, we create attachments and possessions around us, we relate to each other in a physical sense. Within this physical form is our spiritual nature, that combination of intellect and intuition, where we look beyond the physical and feel things that cannot be explained in physical terms.

Love is the essence of our spiritual nature and also of our physical being, as it bridges the gap between the two and fuses them into one. It is an aspiration that all of us harbor deep within us, or, more to the point, it is *the* aspiration we all have deep within us, because it is through love that we come to realize and draw upon the deep connection we have with that Whole, which we call the Universe or God. Love is that central part of us, that core, which is our truest guide to our thoughts and actions: it is our conscience, and also, through the physical mechanism of the heart and the thymus, it is the pulse of our life and our protector.

146

Relationships

Strip away all possessions, all ambition etc., and what are we left with? Our fellow human beings.

We may of course get a temporary sense of pleasure or relief from the material things around us, but the essence of our lives is our relationship with our fellow human beings. It is through our contact with other people that we develop and grow, feel joy and pain. People are the hub and focus of our lives; it is the way in which we choose to relate to them that determines the course of our existence.

I say 'choose', as the way in which we choose to relate to people is the most important fundamental choice in our lives. It is a choice which has a bearing on every aspect of our existence, right down to the physical state of our bodies.

So, how do we define this choice?

I am going to illustrate this by concentrating on what comes first of all to people's minds when they talk about love: that relationship with a special partner. The way in which we handle this relationship is always a perfect reflection of the way in which we relate to people on a much broader scale, even of the way in which we relate to ourselves.

Let us briefly turn to the previous chapter on strength and power, for the barriers which our ego builds between ourselves and other people are what ultimately leads us away from a true understanding of love. For instance, when people talk or sing about love, they are most often referring to two people being 'in love', a state which has very little to do with love in its purest sense.

All of us have been through that state of being 'in love' with someone and many of us still strive to attain that supposed idea. What this expression usually signifies, though, especially in the initial stages of instant attraction, is the process by which we project a fantasy or an image on to the other person – quite often, this image is a reflection of ourselves or of a particular need and we are indeed falling in love with this rather than the person in question.

This brings us to the question of expectation raised earlier – it is a process of our ego and rational mind which divides people up into little parcels, expecting each tiny part to be just right, to fit into place like every piece of a jigsaw. As with all aspects of ego, this view of relationships leads to nothing but limitation. It destroys the infinite possibilities and natural flow that the variety of human relationships can afford us in our lives.

What is more, one cannot live in the state of being 'in love' forever – in day to day existence with a partner, a projected image cannot last, and, if it does, this means that there is no genuine trust and understanding between two people. Ultimately, the image will fall and, as the expectation is shattered, judgment will set in – the person holding on to the image will feel cheated, but, in reality, it is that person who has cheated him or herself.

Judgment, possessiveness, competitiveness, lust, jealousy and much more – are all aspects of ego. Each time we behave and react in this way, we are viewing another person as an extension of ourselves and we are therefore not relating to them as individuals in their own right. Our ego, the focal point of imbalance within the third chakra, is the very antithesis of love, and in being so, draws us away from that highest healing element within us.

Take possessiveness as an example. If you are in a relationship and are inclined to be in the least bit possessive, whether as a lover, parent of friend, what is really going on? You are holding on to the person in question because you are afraid

148

that you will lose this person. In holding on to someone, you are giving into fear and, in doing so, your ego is trying to control this person, rather than letting the person have his or her freedom. If two people are going to be together in a relationship, this will be so because they both choose freely to be together – if one person tries to control and smother another, the natural flow between them is destroyed and the relationship will ultimately die. Possessiveness is the very opposite of trust, and no relationship can survive without trust.

This is so important to understand, as I have seen many people who have been through the harrowing experience of vainly holding on to someone in a relationship way past the time the energy has faded between the two partners. It is of course not easy to let go of someone and face the prospect of being alone, even though you know that the relationship has come to an end; yet the internal damage is even greater if you continue to put your own energy and source of strength out to someone who will give you nothing in return.

Dependence, just like possessiveness, is another form of attachment and is related to this state of expectation and projection of an image. Of course, we all desire a mutually supportive relationship, but there are many who see this support as essential to their existence, where the projection they are imposing on their partner is that of someone stronger than themselves. Such projections have more to do with need than love.

Need and trust are opposites of each other in this respect. A relationship where one partner needs the other in order to feel that he or she is a complete person inevitably puts pressure on the relationship by disturbing the natural balance between two individuals. In feeling a simple sense of trust, on the other hand, two partners acknowledge each other's rights as individuals and, most important of all, understand that each of them is fundamentally responsible for his or her own happiness and well-being.

Acknowledging this individual responsibility enhances rather than detracts from the sharing quality within a relationship, as there is no sense of obligation or pressure. The energy shared between two partners who are at peace within themselves and who trust each other makes that sense of well-being soar to new heights, as the individual strength of each partner feeds the other. And, of course, when one is temporarily down, the other can raise that energy up again.

If, on the other hand, we are talking about a relationship which is built on an image or a need, rather than the deep-rooted connection and flow between two trusting, open spirits, then that relationship will work on exactly the level of the projection. If you are only sharing a part of yourself, or if you allow your partner to share only part of him or herself because you see that partner as an image which does not reflect his or her true self, then the energy shared between you cannot be one of complete harmony and balance – and, ultimately, the cracks will appear.

So often, I have seen a relationship where one person leaves his or her partner for another person and the one left behind wallows in self-pity as the injured party. But do not let yourself be fooled by this; if the energy goes out of a relationship, it is because the connection is no longer or perhaps never has been deep down between the core of these two individuals. If you are honest with yourself, your intuition will always tell you the state of a relationship at any time; so many people intuitively feel a change within a relationship, but are afraid to confront it until it is too late. For we all change, and if you are open with your partner and share these changes, then they do not have to lead you apart.

All of these examples above show how we have subconsciously *chosen* to relate to an individual in a certain way. The way we relate to people on a day to day basis – not just to that special partner, our family or close friends – demonstrates to what level our heart center is truly open. If we find ourselves continuously judging other people or seeing them as extensions of ourselves, then we are still rooted in the center of power. The true energy of love can only flow if we learn to recognize each individual as a complete being

150

unto him or herself.

In failing to understand the meaning of love and thereby failing to have that foundation of love in our lives, we impair the effectiveness of all the physical connections within the heart center: the heart itself, the thymus and the immune system.

The essential question is: 'How deeply and truly do you want to relate?' The honest answer you give is a guide to what love really means to you.

Love: the Great Healer

A relationship can only blossom and grow if it is built on trust. Trust is the ability to open yourself up without reservations or conditions to another person and to see that person as he or she is. This is the basis of love in its clearest and purest sense.

I have just illustrated this in terms of a relationship with a 'special partner', but love works far beyond this limited sphere.

Love is a state of being, not a specific emotion. Remember this. If one lives with love as a state of being throughout one's existence, one will never be seriously sick, as the heart center will remain open and the thymus and immune system will remain active and unimpaired. If you are already sick, then this is the time to understand about love and bring it deep into your being.

Just think for a moment of people, such as Mother Teresa, who radiate nothing but love, and you will begin to understand what love as a state of being means.

Let us start at the beginning again.

Love is concerned only with relating to people, including yourself. All else falls away as irrelevant.

Love has nothing to do with relating to people on a superficial level. You may be with someone as long as you like. You may talk to them, hug them, kiss them, have sex with them, but, unless you really open your heart to them, this has nothing to do with love.

Love starts with yourself. If you are unable to love yourself, you cannot know how to love others. If you are able to see yourself as you are and delight in yourself, then the light is beginning to shine within you.

If you deny yourself love, whether through guilt, fear, self-judgment or a general feeling of lack of worthiness, you are closing down your heart center and the Healer Within. More fundamentally, you are denying yourself that essence within you from which emanates the joy and inner peace that you deserve in every aspect of your life.

Self-love is self-worth, the knowledge that you are worthy of the highest and best in your life and especially worthy of receiving love. If you open yourself to receive love from others, then the love you will give to yourself and to others will increase and increase. Likewise, if you open your heart to others, then you will receive in return, if you accept that you are worthy to do so.

This, in particular, is very important to understand. Love is the balance of giving and receiving and the breaking of that balance can allow dis-ease to enter into your being. I have seen this occur where a person, who is a wonderful warm and loving being, giving of himself to all around him, cannot accept the love offered in return because of a deep down feeling, inspired within him many years back, that he is not worthy of receiving love.

Love just is. It is neutral. Love in its highest form is *perfect balance*. This is why it is the great healer, for, in opening one's spirit, one allows the constant, harmonious flow of light to feed the heart and thymus, bringing health and energy to body and soul.

Love is not the wishy-washy emotion they sing about in love songs; it is a force like a burning arrow that cuts through all the dark and fuzzy aspects of your life. It means delving deep into yourself and into others. Love sees things clearly and truly as they are; if you are at peace with that loving part of yourself, you will see through the masks that others erect around themselves and you will see them as they are. You will see your own and others' true potential.

Love is forgiveness and releasing.

Love is freedom, as it has no ties.

Love is not just going through life being nice and sweet to people. Love and compassion are not to be confused with sympathy. Sympathy is where you enter into the spirit of someone's pain and thereby give it energy; compassion is feeling for someone in their pain, but standing apart from it and guiding that person out of it. Compassion can sometimes appear to be direct, cool and even cruel, but love itself is a cutting force sweeping away all superfluous emotional attachments.

Sympathy for oneself or self-pity, as it is better known, is not showing oneself love, as it is giving energy to one's pain. The healing force of self-love can only be felt if one stands back and rises out of pain and disease, nurturing the creative and loving part of oneself.

You cannot go out looking for love. Love is trusting your instinct in relationships, knowing that, by showing your true self to the world, you will attract towards you those who are of the same energy as yourself, without even having to look for them. Then, there will be no emptiness, no isolation, as you will always have around you those with whom you can share, with whom not even words need be spoken to express the bond of love between you.

But, even more than this, love is an expression of our divine relationship with that almighty Whole, the Universe, which surrounds us wherever we are. It is an expression of the aspiration which we all have deep inside us to live always in peace, harmony and stillness with everything and everyone around us.

It is in that space of stillness that we listen to our inner voice and follow the path of our own individual creativity.

The Fifth Chakra: Communication and Expression

If love is the highest form of spirit on the earthly plane, then expression of this and other aspects of our creativity can only bring the highest feeling of peace and fulfilment within us.

There are so many ways open to us to express our creativity and our highest selves; each one of them lifts us up away from the heavier, lower aspects of ourselves into that realm where we feel the freedom of being at one with ourselves and the world. We can express ourselves through words and touch, singing and dancing, smiling and laughing, to name but a few.

All these means of self-expression and communication are no less open to us when we feel down, for immediate expression of emotion, whether anger or sorrow or grief, is the only way to release it before it is allowed to fester and destroy the balance within. That is why tears are so important, as they are a natural, spontaneous release of sorrow, even sometimes an expression of joy.

In our second chakra, we learn to release our emotions, our sense of limitation and recognize our creativity. In the third, we learn to recognize our inner strength and, in the fourth, we feel the true meaning of love. But, all of this knowledge is worthless if we do not find an outlet for it, a means of expressing it and communicating it to others. The interrelationship which binds this Universe together depends

155

on a continuous flow of communication, from the simple act of a bee pollinating a flower to the interchange of ideas and feelings between two people.

When life seems to be on a downward trend, it is so easy for one to retreat into one's shell. Sometimes, it is necessary to do so in the short term in order to settle into oneself and understand what is going on within; yet, making a habit of this leads to a melancholy within the soul and a gradual withdrawal from the natural energy which constant interchange brings into one's life.

If you are sick, it is all the more tempting to crawl into a dark hole, yet this is actually the time to do the opposite and begin to open yourself up not only to your inner self, but also to the world outside, to the friends who are trying to help you, to the new people in your life whom you meet and who share your predicament.

The challenge of overcoming disease is a true test of your creativity, and creativity cannot be expressed and fulfilled without communication. It is there to be shared and, even though responsibility rests with the individual, the energy between even just two people who share the same goal of banishing disease from their bodies and consciousness doubles the strength of the Healer Within each of them.

For many people, a life-threatening disease presents the first opportunity to stand back from their lives and say: 'I am confronted with the possibility of dying. If I am really going to choose to live, what is it that I really want from this life ahead of me?' And the question itself is a release; it is an act of letting go of the need to hold on to all the superficial rubbish that has for so long drawn energy away from the essence of our lives.

What you are left with is the freedom to express your highest self, to do and to be all the things that you have deep down known to be important to you. It is the time to appreciate your own self-worth, to open your heart up to the world around you and to draw into your sphere and truly communicate with people who are of your nature. Most important of all, it is the time to follow your intuition and do exactly what you *feel* is right, without fear, or self-doubt.

156

The Power of Words

It is amazing how few people really understand the power of words. Words are at the heart of our creativity.

As long as a thought remains in your own mind, it is confined to yourself, your own personal sphere of reference. As soon as this thought is expressed in words, it is released from the confines of your own being and becomes universal.

That is why, even on a day to day basis, I always say: 'Be aware of what you speak.' Within the Universe, there is a natural balance and therefore whatever you put out from your own lips will create a certain reality which will return to you in one way or another. Just look closely at someone who is always finding fault in others and you will see how unharmonious that person's life will be on nearly every level.

We have the gift of communication and that is exactly what he have it for: to communicate. If you use communication for expressing negativity, you are not only wasting that gift, but you are creating an aura of negativity around you which will attract further negativity in your life. Each time you use words to complain about your lot, these words increase the power that this situation has over you. Likewise, if you are constantly 'bitching' about other people, you are giving them power over you and you will continue to attract negative people around you.

Communication is the means we have of relating to people, but it can also be abused to do the contrary. The spoken word can be used as a powerful tool for concealing what is really going on inside you, either through deceit or, more often, the habit of 'making' conversation on a level that has nothing to do with genuine communication.

That is why it is important to feel comfortable with silence. Many people, out of the habit of talking on a superficial level, feel uncomfortable when confronted with even a short period of silence in someone's company. Yet, when you are in the company of someone with whom you feel at ease, silence enables you to communicate on so many different levels – subliminal exchanges which Western man has lost because of his reliance on the spoken word.

As an extension of the way in which we relate to others, the way in which we communicate is a fundamental choice in our lives. If we choose to hide behind our words, we are choosing to suppress our true self with all the imbalance that such a decision brings; if we choose to communicate freely and express our inner selves, then our true nature flows freely outwards and, in joining with others, is reinforced.

The greatest strength of the spoken word is an expression of faith, an affirmation that we can create our own reality. Through the spoken word, we can put out our innermost hopes and desires to connect with that limitless energy within the Universe.

I have already written about faith as the understanding of our link with this Universal Energy and our ability to bring this energy into our own being to create what we choose in our lives. It is through the word that we put this into action.

To give you an idea of the power of words, let us concentrate on two words which have great individual power: Yes and No. We have all seen how a powerful utterance of the word No can have a cowering effect on a dog, but have you ever seen it work in your own life? At any point in the next few days, if you see a situation coming towards you that you do not want to be part of you, just close your eyes, visualize this situation and shout either out loud or powerfully within yourself the word NO.

When you do that, see how the word No creates an energy around it shattering anything in its path.

The word No is a particularly powerful tool in this instance if there is a fear that constantly keeps plaguing your mind. For instance, if you keep on getting an image inside your mind of you becoming sick, launch a NO towards it and see the effect it has. The very way the word is pronounced, in whatever language, has an energy that disrupts anything in its path.

Likewise, the sound of the word Yes has the quality that draws something towards you and it can be used for just that. If there is something which you truly desire and you know is right for you, yet there seem to be too many obstacles around it, then visualize it and put the energy of the word Yes out towards it and see how the obstacles crumble. First of all, you have to know what you truly want or do not want to be part of your life and then you put out the energy of Yes or No to it.

As I previously said, a thought remains in our private sphere until expressed. In verbalizing it, not only do we bring it out into the world, but the process of doing so forces us to transform what may have been a somewhat vague thought in our minds into something that we have to understand and express in a concrete manner. Writing one's thoughts down has a similar effect, which is why I often tell people to keep a journal during periods of profound change. Even writing this book has made me express ideas which were previously only vague concepts.

If you are reading this book, it is likely that you are undergoing a major period of change in your life, so I am going to ask you now to use the power of the spoken word.

MEDITATION NO.9

In your own time, just sit in a quiet place and center yourself. Then, focus on the past and specifically on all those aspects of your life which you do not wish to carry with you into the future. Hopefully, you have by now let go of most people and situations that have caused you pain, but here I wish you also to focus on all those traits in your behavior which you do not like and which you feel limit your ability to create your own reality.

As you say out loud: 'I let go of . . . and do not want it to be part of my life again', you understand exactly what it is that you are releasing and you see that limitation pour out of your being.

You continue to do this until everything is exhausted and you can even write these things down as you identify them – the act of doing this often creates connections in your mind and makes you think of something else that lies hidden.

Once you are satisfied that you have covered all that needs to be covered, just let your mind go blank and focus on your present self.

Then, gradually allow to come to the surface the most important, the deepest aspirations and desires you have for the present and the future. One by one, see them within you and speak them out loud, affirming that they will happen. And each time an image of yourself in a creative guise comes to your mind, affirm this deepest part of you with the words: I AM.

Whatever it is that you are asking for which will point you towards your highest potential, you do it with the faith that, in putting it out to the Universe, the Universe will provide through its intricate, infinite connections. And if you have doubts about the effectiveness of such affirmations, then put it out there that you may learn faith and learn to accept that it is your God given right to have harmony, stillness, joy and love in your life.

The Sixth Chakra:
the Rational
and the Intuitive

Despite these doubts, deep down you feel that this natural balance and harmony in the world is right and can be drawn upon into your own life – it is your rational mind that has the doubt. Nothing that I write will be of any worth to you unless it feels right – and even the sense of it feeling right may be submerged by that rational part of you that needs tangible proof of everything before you accept it.

As I come to the end of this book, I am going to spend a little time explaining the essence of those two seemingly opposite sides of us: the rational and the intuitive. The way in which we allow one to dominate the other is probably the most fundamental imbalance within us, which filters down into all the other aspects of our behavior – remember how I wrote about the pituitary and pineal glands at the beginning of the book and how they basically control all the other parts of the endocrine system below them.

From his early origins as a creature of instinct, man's rational faculties have grown at an ever increasing rate to reach their peak at the time we are in now. But, what exactly is this thing which we call the rational mind?

I prefer to call it the sequential mind as the key to its growth is sequence: as man sees and understands one part of his existence, this leads him to an understanding of the next stage. What the sequential mind is in fact doing is taking each part of the Whole which is the Universe and dividing it up into little parcels of knowledge which our limited faculties can grasp. In doing so, man started by first being able to understand individual parts of this whole, his environment, until this understanding of it gradually increased to the point where he can now even harness and alter parts of it.

This is seeing the rational, sequential mind from a global standpoint. Of much more relevance to dis-ease and health is the way in which the development of the rational mind affects us on a personal level, in particular with regard to the way we relate to the world around us.

From an early age, most of us are sent to school, following an education which is designed almost exclusively to develop our rational faculties. Whether in mathematics and science or history and economics, we are given specific pieces of information to learn and then to relate to each other. Our so-called intelligence is judged on our ability to absorb these countless bits of information, and, as we grow older, our 'usefulness' in the world is in turn judged by this 'intelligence'.

In dividing everything we do, see or experience into so many different and often seemingly unrelated little parcels, it is not surprising that our minds are never still or that you hear people so often say: 'Oh! I never seem to have time to sit down and relax.' This constant darting of the mind from one thing to another is probably the most common addiction of the urbanized Western world – an addiction it certainly is, as it is a means of giving up one's power by constantly worrying about and putting energy into a whole diversity of things that have no real, deep bearing on our lives. In addition, the impatience which arises from this state of mind never allows one to truly settle within that stillness, that giving and receiving state of being which I described as love earlier on.

As you might have imagined, this leads me back once more to that same old question of balance. If you are a person whose mind is never at rest and needs constantly to be occupied doing or worrying about something, you not only create tension and stress which affects the whole of your endocrine system. Of even more importance is the fact that you are constantly drawing energy out of yourself away from that true essence within you, denying that essential intuitive half of your mind and leaving emptiness in its place.

So, what is intuition?

In contrast to the rational mind, which divides everything into little pieces and must have explanations for everything, our intuitive mind is that part of us which sees and accepts the Whole. The rational mind is active, always doing; the intuitive mind is passive and receptive. The intuitive mind is what we call instinct, whereby we do things spontaneously without conscious thought. It is that part of us from where we get thoughts out of the blue and we wonder where they came from!

The most elemental example of the intuitive mind common to all living creatures is the survival instinct. As a species, man has always been a social animal, so the importance we place on relationships in our lives is also a fundamental instinct. Yet, what is most relevant to us here is the intuitive part of us which is particular to each one of us, which creates our own individuality.

Our individuality is of course partly created by the accumulation of experiences throughout our lives, but there is something more to it than that, a vague quality within each person which is distinguishable from any other person.

This is the intuitive part of an individual which resides in the sixth chakra, the third eye, and which rises up through the seventh, the crown chakra to connect with the Whole, the limitless energy and order of God, the Universe. As with those thoughts that come to us out of the blue, this connection is what makes us feel when things are right, as the information and thoughts we receive in this manner come from a source which sees the whole picture. Instead of the limited view of reality seen by our rational mind, our intuitive mind guides us in a direction, which goes far beyond the scope of our understanding, towards our highest potential – a potential which we may at this point in our lives not be able to comprehend. In the case of a serious disease, this at first sight seems to mean nothing but pain and suffering, yet it has the potential, if you follow the strength of your intuition, to open a whole new vision of life for you.

This is why faith and intuition are inextricably bound together – in trusting your intuition, you have faith that this is your connection to the Universe which will guide you to your highest good in all that you do.

And this in turn is why I always say to people, especially in these times: 'Always follow your intuition'. Every so often, something will come to your mind that just feels right: a feeling that you should embark on a new course in whatever aspect of your life, a feeling so strong that you cannot avoid making a decision.

The important thing is that, if you feel something strongly enough, you should do it. It is fairly inevitable that, along with this intuitive feeling, your rational mind will come up with lots of little objections, such as 'It's too risky', 'What will people think?' or 'My doctors would not approve'.

Well, the ultimate question is: do you wish to live the rest of your life in fear and through the eyes of others or do you wish to be yourself and follow that inner part of yourself? Just another choice!

It may appear that what I am doing here is exalting the intuitive over the rational mind, but this is not the case.

In our modern, 'civilized' world, the behavior of most people is governed ninety per cent by the rational mind and ten per cent by the intuitive mind. What I am saying is that we should allow the intelligence of our rational understanding to be at one with our spiritual nature. We should learn to recognize when our intuition is tapping into the broader picture which our rational mind cannot see.

On a physiological level, this is what the right and left side of the brain are all about and it is the cerebral cortex which links the two so that they can work together. And (you must be getting rather bored of this word by now!), what about balance? Right at the beginning of this book, I wrote about the pineal and pituitary glands, which are the masters of the endocrine system. Quite simply, if there is balance within this sphere of our being, then balance and health will reign in the rest of our body.

So, you may ask, if balance between intuition and rationality will bring the rest of the body into balance, why bother with the rest of the book? The answer, and you will see as you look at your own behavior, is that all these things we have been letting go of, from fear to guilt, jealousy to judgment, are all products of a rational mind devoid of intuitive input. They are all aspects of our lives which have been parcelled off and have been given a surplus of energy, taking away from the natural energy, flow and balance of the whole.

Throughout this book, I have been suggesting meditations which have all been fairly specific. This final one is what I call the 'Maintenance Meditation'. It is, by and large, what I do every day both in the morning and the evening, and, once you get used to it, it need only take ten minutes.

It may be that you already do your own regular meditation, which is fine. This is for people who wish to get started, but I always say that you must in the end follow whatever feels right for you.

The essence of meditation is to bring stillness into your life at the beginning and end of every day. If this book has at all changed your perception of life, or if changes are happening to you anyway, it is so important to make a point at least twice a day of calmly entering your own space and just being there within yourself.

To begin with, meditation can be a bit of a struggle, as your mind will keep hopping in lots of different directions. This does not matter. Just be aware of yourself doing this, let go of whatever distracting thought you have and return to that central part of yourself. Do not fight it. In the end, it will become second nature, and the freshness and lightness you will feel after just a few minutes of inner peace will be something you can draw upon at any time of the day.

In the summer and whenever I can, I will always do my meditation leaning against a tree trunk, as this really gives me a sense of connection with the earth, but the important thing is to choose a place which is as quiet as possible. I also find that sitting as erect as possible always helps – otherwise, I have a tendency to doze off!

MEDITATION NO.10

You begin this meditation by closing your eyes and then grounding and running your energies in exactly the way that I described in Meditation No.1 at the beginning of the book. Once you are comfortable with this, instead of opening your eyes, you continue as follows.

What you are going to do first of all is to visualize your chakras. At first this may be a little difficult but, once you have a feel of them, it will come to you very easily. It may even be that visualizing them is not right for you – it may be better to sense their position in your body and feel the different currents of energy in these parts of your body.

In a visual sense, your chakras are like whirlpools or tornados of energy starting off at their widest point two inches away from the body and at the narrowest point attached to the spinal cord.

Your first chakra is attached to your coccyx bone at the base of your spine and faces downwards towards the earth. At its widest point, two inches from the body, it is about the width of a golf ball.

Your second chakra is situated two fingers' width below your navel. It is attached to the spinal cord at that level and faces outwards two inches in front of your body – at its widest point, it is about the width of a tennis ball.

Your third chakra is located in the solar plexus area just beneath the breastbone and is the same size as the second.

Your fourth chakra is at the level of your heart, although, unlike the heart itself, it is in the central part of you attached to your spinal cord. It is the same size as the second and third.

Your fifth is located in your throat and is about the size of the first.

Your sixth is in the central part of your forehead just above the eyebrows and is the same size, maybe a little smaller, than the fifth.

Your seventh points upwards to the sky above you connecting to that central part of the brain, and, at its widest point two inches above the body, is about the size of the rim of a coffee mug.

You focus on these seven chakras and see or feel them all aligned in a straight line along your spinal cord.

Then, you concentrate on the three lower chakras and see a narrow, hollow cord stretch out from each of them all the way from the spine out into the distance.

Focusing in turn on the first, second and third, you see a brilliant gold light shooting towards your body from some point in the distance and this in turn enters each of your three lower chakras. As this bright light energy comes flowing into each chakra, it disturbs all the dark mass, like a thick layer of grime and dust, which has been allowed to accumulate there over the years – in the second, this black grime represents all the emotional charges that you have been hanging on to all these years and, in the third, it is all the imbalance of power, guilt and judgment etc. that you have allowed to build up inside you.

And, as this gold light breaks up this dark, life-less energy inside you, it sweeps all the darkness out

from inside you through the hollow cord attached to your chakra and out into the universe. So, as the light initially spreads into your chakra, the light that comes out through the cord is darkened by this layer upon layer of dirt being swept out with it. As the light continues to pour in and more and more heaviness is swept away, the light leaving through the cord gradually becomes brighter and brighter until it is just as bright as the gold light coming in. Then, all the dark energy has been swept away.

Once you have finished this to your satisfaction, you let the cords just slip away into the distance and see and feel each of those lower aspects of yourself filled with a new light energy.

Then, you focus on your upper four chakras and repeat the process. As the light flows into your heart chakra, you feel being expelled all those parts of you which say that you are not worthy of love and which prevent you from giving love out to others. As it becomes clearer, you feel the whole energy of your heart expand, not just from the light from outside, but also, now that it has been freed, that true essence of yourself which is and always will be within, flowing through every aspect of your being. When you finally allow the cords to disappear and the gold light to fade, there comes from within an image of a beautiful pink rose which radiates its own loving energy throughout your being, filling your whole body with life and energy, stimulating your heart and immune system, radiating health in every cell and destroying any foreign body or virus which does not belong there.

When you are satisfied that your whole body is radiating with this energy of light, you move up to your throat center and see the gold light pouring in, not only clearing out all those ties that prevent you from expressing your true creativity, but also spreading down your arms to your fingertips filling them with the light and energy of creativity. And, as you have expelled all the darkness from this fifth chakra, you allow the cord and the gold light to fade away and, from within, streams out a blue light, the ray of communication which is that natural expressive part of you.

You then move up to your third eye, and, as the gold light pours in, you see it expand, and as the light passes through the opening, it enters what seems like an enormous cavern stretching far beyond the imaginings of your own mind. This dark cavern becomes brighter and brighter, larger and larger as the light continues to flow in through your third eye, until there seem to be no walls to this cavern, only a ceiling. And, as you look above you, you see this ceiling burst open with a flash of light entering from above through your Crown Chakra, combining the limitless knowledge and energy of the Universe with that space, which is your own individuality. And you feel yourself standing in the middle of this limitless light and space around you, knowing that this is the energy which is there both within and outside you, the two fusing together, to be drawn into your being at will.

As you feel this energy, you see your body in your mind's eye and, as you breathe deeply, you see the light that is radiating within it expand two feet beyond the contours of your physical body. You allow that energy of light, your own space, to remain there knowing that it is there to protect you from any outside force which does not belong to your being.

So, for a while, you just sit there, allowing this freedom, this essential energy of light within you, to become familiar to you.

Then, finally, you open your eyes and put your hands down on the ground to let any excess energy flow out into the earth.

Postcript

I am sure you have by now heard the term: 'The New Age'.
I am not so wild about such specific terms myself, but the
truth is that we have entered into a period of change on this
planet which has not occurred to this extent for thousands
of years. I am not talking about material and technological
change, although this is all part of it; I am referring to a
fundamental shift in Consciousness.

The old age was the Age of Pisces and the figure who
introduced this age in the West was Jesus Christ, Christ the
Fisherman. He, like Buddha and others before him, was a
prophet, teacher and healer of immense statute, and, if you
strip down the dogma which has been added to his life and
words since he left this planet, he taught two very basic
things: 'God is Love' and 'God is Within You'.

His life and actions were, in a sense, a spark, a legacy laid
down for us living in the world today. Following his death,
the world became enmeshed in a vibration, where power,
manipulation and control have ever since been the essential
hallmarks of our behavior, especially of the behavior of our
leaders.

The 'organized' religions of today have sadly led the
way in this respect and have much to answer for, as they so
imperiously set themselves up as the keepers of the spiritual
side of man. From as early as the fourth century AD when
the Roman Emperor Constantine espoused Christianity for

political reasons, the hierarchy of the Christian Church has often been more interested in power than love. (Of course, Christianity has been the inspiration of some of the most blessed, influential figures in our history, but their inspiration came from an *individual* faith and sense of purpose.)

It is a constant source of amazement to me how organized religion continues to pour energy into negativity and hate rather than focus on good and love. For so many of my generation, religion means nothing because the spirit has been taken out of it. The Catholic Church spends all its energy on sin and guilt; the so-called 'Fundamentalists' preach a regime of intolerance and self-righteousness. This has nothing to do with Spirit; it has everything to do with power.

I have mentioned this perversion of Christ's teaching here, because this 'New Age' into which we have entered is basically a renewal of that spark which may be called the True Christ Consciousness, where each individual finds the God within him or herself.

To those of you for whom the words Christ and Christianity have bad or even absurd connotations, let me explain what I mean by the Christ Consciousness. The word Christ was a term used to describe the human being we know as Jesus, but is not inseparable from Jesus. It is a Consciousness – Jesus happened to be at that time in history the vehicle for spreading the teachings of this Consciousness. Therefore, the return of the Christ Consciousness has nothing to do with the man Jesus; it is the return of his very simple teachings which have been forgotten: 'God is Love' and 'God is Within'. In other words, it means that the Earth and Mankind, as the highest form of Consciousness on the Earth, will raise themselves out of the power vibration into the vibration of love, out of the third chakra into our rightful place of the fourth chakra, the center of the heart.

So, what does all this mean in terms of us as individuals?

On the personal level, the beginning of a new age or cycle is always heralded in by an incredible surge of energy into people's lives and the planet as a whole – an energy which makes the impetus for change and inner transformation stronger and stronger.

This energy has been gradually increasing for quite a few years, but in particular burst through in the middle of 1987, and will continue at this pace for quite a few years to come.

By the time you read this book, that energy will have become like a giant booster rocket behind you – as a 'channel' friend of mine so aptly described it to me recently, the change of energy we are going through is like taking out a 40 watt bulb and replacing it with a 200 watt bulb.

This is why the process of letting go is so important. This surge of energy which is sweeping through our lives at this moment is so powerful that, if we are light with no attachments and encumbrances, we shall be swept along with it to the extent that we cannot imagine how much our lives will have been transformed within even a few years from now – not only in terms of the potential within us, but also in terms of the ease and peace which will fill our lives. If, on the other hand, we still have excess baggage on us, we are in for a bumpy ride, knocking our heads continuously on the obstacles we create for ourselves.

That is why it is so important to get to the point of releasing all this superfluous crap in your lives and learning to distinguish that voice of true intuition from the voice of fear. The choice is so simple: in following your intuition, your life will speed on; in giving in to doubt and fear, in holding on to the past, these changes will pass you by. It does not matter if you do not know where these changes will lead you; if you are patient and follow that intuitive part of you, it will be made perfectly clear in time.

So many people have said to me: 'What is so special about us? Aren't we being a bit arrogant and unrealistic to believe that we are going to herald such a change in the world when life has been this way as long as history remembers?' My reply is always that this is something you can only answer for yourself. If you feel that you do have something to contribute to the world which will move this transformation forwards, then it is so. Only if you feel it within yourself can it be so.

The period of time we are entering into is literally *what we have all been waiting for*. It sounds a bit simplistic, doesn't it? But, there has been an incredible sense of anticipation building up for so long, often subconsciously, within so many people and these changes are the fruition of that feeling. I can hardly keep count of the people I meet on a day to day basis in the most unlikely circumstances who have had this feeling awaken inside them recently and only need someone to express it to, in order to share it. People are crawling out of the woodwork, understanding that a time for change in the way we behave towards each other has come: a time for Love. And, if you acknowledge and freely express that spiritual, loving side of your nature, you too will continuously be drawn to others who are undergoing the same changes.

Like a wounded animal trapped in a corner, the old way will fight to preserve itself and, over the next five years at least, there will still be conflict to the degree that any talk of a loving world may seem absurdly unrealistic. But, it will be the death throes of the Old Age.

What is important is to just let this be and understand that it has nothing to do with you; to fight, to judge, to get involved in global conflict will only be to give it energy. The important thing is for us all to live our own lives according to our hearts and conscience and intuition; by residing within that core of inner strength and cutting through intolerance and hate within our own sphere of influence, we allow the light of that Consciousness of Love to emanate into the hearts of others, spreading and growing until there is no room in the world for the consciousness of power.

Again, if you feel that this is unrealistic, you have not taken in what this book is all about: responsibility. Not only do we have responsibility for our own lives; accepting that responsibility means that we are accepting responsibility for change within the world as a whole. If you say with a tone of defeat: 'What can I do to change the world?', you are denying that system of interrelationships, of eternal connections which makes up our Universe.

You have no doubt heard of the 'Domino' theory. Well, it does not have to refer to one country after the other falling under the 'spell of Communism'; it refers more relevantly to one individual changing another changing another changing another – ultimately changing the mass of humanity. And, of course, it is not just happening in your own back yard; this new awareness, this new consciousness is raising its head everywhere, quietly at first, but soon to have the force of a tidal wave.

And you know it!

One final word.

As you awaken to your own higher consciousness, it is a natural progression that you will be drawn to others and meet, seemingly by chance, people who are going through the same process.

You may feel that you need some guidance and you will find that there will be no shortage of teachers.

Remember two things. First of all: 'God is Within'. A teacher can only take you so far, and, in the end, you have to find your own way by listening to the voice within.

Secondly: choose your teacher carefully. If you feel you need one, following your intuition as to who is right for you. Do not immediately accept one because someone you know has done so. This person may be a wonderful teacher, but the important thing is that he or she must be of your energy, must feel right for you.

And beware – (I hate to sound like a prophet of doom, but this is a necessary warning) – of false teachers. If you come across one who says that his or hers is the only way, or if you find that this person has allowed to build around him or her a circle of admirers, then stay clear. I have come across quite a few – they are still in the power vibration; they are not coming from the egoless state of Love.

So, I hope and trust that this book will be a vehicle for

change in your life, so that you may enter into a new world of your own inner strength, love and, of course, peace, happiness and laughter.

If you have anything you wish to write to me about, which seems unclear, please do not hesitate to do so, c/o Amethyst Books, and I shall write back as soon as I can.